Cambridge Elements ≡

Elements in Evolutionary Economics
edited by
John Foster
University of Queensland
Jason Potts
RMIT University

T0286161

EVOLUTIONARY ECONOMICS

Its Nature and Future

Geoffrey M. Hodgson
Loughborough University London

CAMBRIDGE
UNIVERSITY PRESS

CAMBRIDGE
UNIVERSITY PRESS

University Printing House, Cambridge CB2 8BS, United Kingdom

One Liberty Plaza, 20th Floor, New York, NY 10006, USA

477 Williamstown Road, Port Melbourne, VIC 3207, Australia

314–321, 3rd Floor, Plot 3, Splendor Forum, Jasola District Centre, New Delhi – 110025, India

79 Anson Road, #06–04/06, Singapore 079906

Cambridge University Press is part of the University of Cambridge.

It furthers the University's mission by disseminating knowledge in the pursuit of education, learning, and research at the highest international levels of excellence.

www.cambridge.org
Information on this title: www.cambridge.org/9781108738002
DOI: 10.1017/9781108767811

First published 2019

A catalogue record for this publication is available from the British Library.

ISBN 978-1-108-73800-2 Paperback
ISSN 2514-3573 (online)
ISSN 2514-3581 (print)

Evolutionary Economics

Its Nature and Future

Elements in Evolutionary Economics

DOI: 10.1017/9781108767811
First published online: July 2019

Geoffrey M. Hodgson
Loughborough University London

Author for correspondence: Geoffrey M. Hodgson, geoff@vivarais.co.uk

Abstract: This Element examines the historical emergence of evolutionary economics, its development into a strong research theme after 1980, and how it has hosted a diverse set of approaches. Its focus on complexity, economic dynamics, and bounded rationality is underlined. Its core ideas are compared with those of mainstream economics. But while evolutionary economics has inspired research in a number of areas in business studies and social science, these have become specialized and fragmented. Evolutionary economics lacks a sufficiently developed core theory that might promote greater conversation across these fields. A possible unifying framework is generalized Darwinism. Stronger links could also be made with other areas of evolutionary research, such as with evolutionary anthropology and evolutionary psychology. As evolutionary economics has migrated from departments of economics to business schools, institutes of innovation studies, and elsewhere, it also needs to address the problem of its lack of a single disciplinary location within academia.

ISBNs: 9781108738002 (PB), 9781108767811 (OC)
ISSNs: 2514-3573 (online), 2514-3581 (print)

Contents

1 Introduction

Historically, a number of approaches in economics, including varied works by Adam Smith, Karl Marx, Carl Menger, Alfred Marshall, Thorstein Veblen, Joseph Schumpeter, and Friedrich Hayek, have all been described as 'evolutionary'. This is understandable, because 'evolutionary' is a broad word, loosely denoting a concern with transformation, innovation, and development.

But today the term 'evolutionary economics' is more typically associated with a new wave of theorising signalled by the seminal work of Richard Nelson and Sidney Winter in their *An Evolutionary Theory of Economic Change* (1982). Although there is not yet any consensus on core principles, this wave of evolutionary thinking has given rise to a number of policy developments and has proved to be influential in several sub-disciplines, in business schools, and in institutions concerned with science and innovation policy.

Citation and other bibliometric studies show that modern evolutionary economics, despite its internal diversity, has created a global network of identifiable, interacting researchers. This Element turns to theoretical ideas and it outlines some of the shared basic assumptions of this broad approach. It also addresses the possibility of the creation of a shared theoretical framework based on generalised Darwinian principles. Further sections compare evolutionary economics with mainstream economics and with evolutionary game theory.

Another notable difference between evolutionary economics and mainstream and game-theoretic genres is that the former gives greater relative emphasis to appreciative (i.e., non-formalised and empirically oriented) theorising. Mathematical and statistical techniques are still widely used in this field, but there is less concentration on full analytic solutions and more on illustrative simulations including agent-based modelling, with attempts to explain real empirical phenomena. The concluding section to this Element considers the prospects for evolutionary economics in the future.

The term 'evolutionary economics' is applied to a diverse set of approaches that vary widely in terms of their basic assumptions, their distances from mainstream economics, their attitudes to Darwinian ideas from biology, and their range of policy conclusions. The historical sources and nature of some of these divergences will be explored later. This diversity results in part from the fact that 'evolution' is a vague word with a variety of meanings.

Despite this diversity, there are common themes among economists who describe themselves as evolutionary. There is a common emphasis on matters of economic change and transformation. Typically, evolutionary economists do not take institutions or technology as given: they treat them as costly to produce and focus on how they emerge and develop. They have a shared interest in novelty and innovation. Evolutionary economists also generally assume that complex phenomena do not often emerge by design. As in nature, complex phenomena frequently result from processes of self-organisation and competitive selection.

This Element examines the historical roots of evolutionary economics and then elaborates on its shared concerns and ideas. A further section establishes a simple taxonomy of differences within this stream of research. A subsequent selection considers recent work on shared evolutionary principles. Further sections elaborate on differences between evolutionary and mainstream economics and make comparisons between evolutionary economics and evolutionary game theory (Hodgson and Huang 2012). The final section considers the prospects for evolutionary economics in the twenty-first century.

2 The Emergence of Modern Evolutionary Economics

Etymologically, 'evolution', like the word 'development', stems from the Latin verb *volvere*. This means 'to roll' but it can refer more broadly to the general idea of motion. The companion verbs *evolvere* and *revolvere* are more explicit, respectively denoting forward and backward motion, as in the unrolling and rolling up of a scroll. The word 'evolution' therefore derives from a Latin word associated with a specifically directional and predestined activity; the scroll is unrolled to reveal that which is already written within.

In this spirit the word 'evolution' was first applied to natural phenomena by the German biologist Albrecht von Haller in 1744. He used the term to characterise embryological development as the augmentation and expansion of a preformed miniature adult organism, which was a common idea in the seventeenth and eighteenth centuries. In biology, the idea of preformation, where the embryo is deemed to contain in microcosm the form of its future development, lasted well into the nineteenth century, being embraced explicitly by Herbert Spencer and more subtly affecting Charles Darwin's thought (Richards 1992).

Spencer was a hugely influential nineteenth-century evolutionary theorist, and he did much more than Darwin to popularize the term 'evolution'. Spencer also coined the phrase 'survival of the fittest', which Darwin adopted only sporadically. Spencer (1862, p. 216) defined evolution in terms of a single system and its 'change from an indefinite, incoherent homogeneity, to a definite, coherent heterogeneity through continuous differentiations'. Hence, instead of natural selection, Spencer appealed to a supposed, unexplained, universal law that led somehow to greater complexity.

Spencer was inspired by Jean-Baptiste de Lamarck (1963), who in 1809 had similarly proposed increasing complexity as a law of evolution. Spencer also adopted Lamarck's proposal that acquired characters could be inherited. Darwin also thought that the inheritance of acquired characters is possible, but he saw this as a matter of empirical investigation rather than a universal law.

In the first edition of the *Origin of Species,* Darwin did not use the word 'evolution' and wrote 'evolved' only once. Subsequently he infrequently used the term 'evolution', but on the whole he preferred phrases like 'descent with modification'. Hence no Darwinian copyright can be imposed on the word 'evolution': it is not of Darwinian provenance.

The history of the word 'evolution' and of 'evolutionary' ideas in the natural and social sciences shows that these terms have been used in very different ways, and there is no historical basis to give them one particular meaning. Today 'evolution' is used in a number of senses, and there is little basis to claim that any one has greater legitimacy than the others. Attempts to give evolution some narrower and sharper meaning, whether Darwinian or otherwise, are unwarranted and unlikely to be successful.

Marx's economics has been described as evolutionary because it depicts history as going through a series of stages, namely from primitive society, through ancient civilisations, feudalism, and capitalism, and finally to communism. History thus unrolls in a Hegelian manner. Clearly this notion of evolution is redolent of the Latin *evolvere,* but it is a conception of change that differs greatly from Darwin's, as Thorstein Veblen (1906, 1907) astutely observed.

The first known use of the term 'evolutionary economics' in English was by Veblen (1898, p. 398). He gave this term a particular connotation that has not been widely adopted since. Veblen (1899, 1919) argued that economics should become 'post-Darwinian' and embody the insights of Darwinian evolutionary theory. He was one of the first to uphold that selection processes operated on institutions in society as well as organisms in nature: institutions as well as individuals were objects of selection (Camic and Hodgson 2011).

Although Veblen was one of the founders of the original institutional economics, his followers quickly abandoned his Darwinian legacy (Hodgson 2004a, Rutherford 2011). By the 1920s any appeal to ideas from biology had become extremely unpopular in all Anglophone social sciences. Even when Veblen's followers retained the word 'evolutionary', it was used to refer more broadly to development and change, and mostly without any Darwinian connotations. This was the case in the USA with the Association for Evolutionary Economics (AFEE), which was founded in 1966. Like Nelson and Winter

(1982) and their 'neo-Schumpeterian' followers, AFEE invoked the term 'evolutionary' without any explicit appeal to Darwinian ideas.

Clarence Ayres was the leading intellectual influence over AFEE at its formation. Ayres (1932, p. 95) was rather dismissive of Darwinism. He had written that 'Darwin's "particular views" have gone down wind: variation, survival of the fittest, natural selection, sexual selection, and all the rest. Darwin is very nearly, if not quite, as outmoded today as Lamarck.' Ayres (1932, p. 234) promoted an interpretation in which 'evolution means the general theory of development without reference to particular mechanism of variation, selection or what not'. Generally, Ayres's views were very influential among original institutional economists in the post-1945 period. Consequently, Veblen's appeal for a 'post-Darwinian' economics was largely ignored, even among his followers.[1]

For a while, Schumpeter (1934, pp. 57–8) saw the term 'evolution' as 'discredited'. Later he adopted the term himself (Schumpeter 1939, 1942), but he never interpreted evolution in Darwinian terms (Hodgson 1993, Witt 2002). Yet he made analyses of technical change, entrepreneurship, and innovation the centrepieces of his work. He saw static analysis of circular flow as a limiting case and upheld the primary quest to understand the processes of restless dynamism and transformation. Work influenced by Schumpeter is also described as 'evolutionary economics' as evidenced by the title of *Journal of Evolutionary Economics*, published by the International Joseph Schumpeter Society.

Another strand of evolutionary thinking originates within the Austrian school of economists, particularly Carl Menger, Ludwig von Mises, and Friedrich Hayek. Menger's (1871) theory of the emergence of money is often cited as evolutionary because it is an attempt to understand the emergence of an institution. But evolutionary discourse in Austrian economists was much more developed in the case of Hayek (1967, 1973, 1979, 1988). He made use of notions of evolutionary selection and drew parallels between evolution in society and evolution in the natural world. But while Hayek acknowledged Darwin and used the Darwinian idea of selection, he saw Darwinism as one stage in a long, vaguely defined line of 'evolutionary' thinking rather than an intellectual revolution in its own right (Hodgson 1993).

Given the rather broad and vague set of concerns that have been described as 'evolutionary' and the wide usage of the term, we cannot object when other writers identify 'evolutionary' themes in various writers including Adam Smith,

---

[1] Jones (1995, p. 419) argued that 'Ayres simply failed to come to effective grips with Darwin's work'. Similar criticisms of Ayres's view of Darwinism are found in Hodgson (2004a).

Karl Marx, Carl Menger, and Alfred Marshall. Evolution is a broad word, and it invokes lots of different ideas. There is nothing wrong with that. It would be a mistake to infer that 'evolution' implies a clear set of principles or inherently means Darwinian. The relevance, or otherwise, of Darwinian ideas for economics and other social sciences has to be established by evidence and argument, not simply by a semantic claim that evolution necessarily implies Darwinism or any other particular theoretical framework.

A number of works prepared the ground for the surge of evolutionary thinking in the 1980s. Hayek's prescient works in the 1970s have already been noted. Nicholas Georgescu-Roegen (1971) introduced the entropy law into economic theory and also made bridges between some types of evolutionary analysis and ecological economics. János Kornai (1971) developed a highly innovative and dynamic theoretical approach. Also, Kenneth Boulding (1981) produced a treatise entitled *Evolutionary Economics*.

But the strongest boost came with the publication of Richard Nelson's and Sidney Winter's (1982) *Evolutionary Theory of Economic Change*. Their line of research originated in the RAND organisation and was there inspired by Armen Alchian (1950). Nelson and Winter were also influenced by Schumpeter's (1934, 1942) emphasis on innovation and dynamics, Hayek's (1948) stress on the role of knowledge, Herbert Simon's (1957) ideas on satisficing and bounded rationality, and the behavioural theory of the firm (Cyert and March 1963).

Since 1980 theoretical developments in evolutionary economics have been significant, and a huge amount of related material has been published, but as yet there has been no convergence on an integrated approach (Silva and Teixeira 2009). Despite the field's internal heterogeneity and lack of consensus on key issues, the networks, journals, and forums that developed after the 1980s created a scattered but linked community of scholars addressing common problems and overlapping research agendas. The scholars were also united by their common dislike of the static and equilibrium approaches that dominated mainstream economics.

By the 1990s it was possible to write of an international network or 'invisible college' of evolutionary economists who, despite their analytical differences, were focusing on the problem of analysing structural, technological, cultural, and institutional change in economic systems (Verspagen and Werker 2003, Witt 2008, Silva and Teixeira 2009). Reference within this informal college is typically made to a variety of alleged precursors such as Schumpeter, Hayek, Marshall, and Veblen, but the evolutionary college is too amorphous and eclectic to warrant a description in terms of a single mentor.

There are also potential links with research programmes that originated outside economics. Among these is the 'organisational ecology' approach

(Hannan and Freeman 1989), work on organisational adaption (Levinthal 1992), and other work of an evolutionary nature in organisation studies (Aldrich and Ruef 2006).

Post-1980 evolutionary economics has also been prominent in various policy debates, particularly concerning policies for technological development, innovation, and business strategy (Dosi *et al.* 1988, Lundvall 1992, Nelson 1993, McKelvey 1996, Murman 2003). Its influence is generally stronger in business schools and other applied research institutions than in university departments of economics. Nevertheless, policy work emanating from evolutionary economics ranges from advocacy of major state interventions in the economy to vigilant support of free-market policies.

3 Evolutionary and Mainstream Economics Compared

Although differences exist within evolutionary economics on many theoretical and practical questions, we can conceive of a paradigm shift fuelled by insights from both evolutionary and institutional thinking. Figure 1 maps the landscape of theoretical depictions of individual interactions in economics. Both axes concern theories about the world, rather than the world itself. The horizontal dimension refers to the minimum number of actors in the theory concerned. The vertical dimension refers to the assumed extent of knowledge and deliberative (rational) consideration of the (rational) deliberation and knowledge of other individual actors in the theory.

Starting with the bottom-left corner of the figure, simple monopoly refers to elementary monopoly theory – without price discrimination – where the monopolist merely faces an aggregate demand curve, and individual consumers do

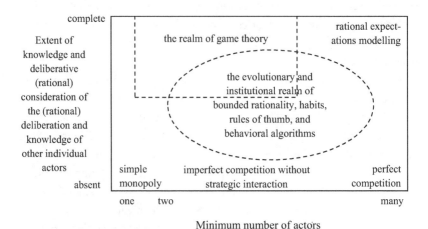

Figure 1 A landscape of economic theory

not otherwise come into the picture. In the bottom-right corner, perfect competition beholds the price-taking competitive firm of the textbooks. For most of the twentieth century, economic theory explored the linear region at the bottom of this diagram, between simple monopoly and perfect competition, including early theories of imperfect competition without strategic interaction.

Rational expectations modelling appears in the top-right corner of the figure. These models assume that agents through experience quickly become aware of the 'true' underlying model of the economy. Assuming a sufficient number of other competing agents who are all similarly informed, the well-known result is that government macroeconomic policy is ineffective. The rationality assumptions, however, are universal and extreme. It is widely known that this result does not hold up with even partial relaxations of these assumptions, such as the introduction of heterogeneous agents who vary in their information-processing capabilities (Haltiwanger and Waldman, 1985).

The widespread adoption of game theory in the 1980s (although it had much earlier precedents in the works of Augustin Cournot and Joseph Bertrand) led economists into new territory. Strategic interactions were considered with a limited number of actors, often with the 'common knowledge of rationality' assumption that not only are individuals rational but also everyone believes that all others will act rationally. Long reasoning chains like 'if I think that she thinks that I think … ' emerge, often creating intractable logical problems of self-reference and infinite regress (Hargreaves Heap and Varoufakis, 1995).

Game theory occupies an upper region in the diagram. Note that the realm of game theory extends downwards to some extent into an area where agents are assumed to take partial but incomplete account of the strategic deliberations of others. This lower area within the game theory box includes behavioural game theory (Camerer 2003).

In the central region of the diagram, between game theory and the monopoly-competition axis at the bottom, lies the realm of modern evolutionary and institutional economics. Like game theory it assumes a structured world of limited interconnectedness, dominated by rules. Unlike much game theory, it adopts a more limited view of individual deliberative and calculative capacities. Decision-making takes place in the context of complexity and radical uncertainty, limiting the chains of logical reasoning concerning the likely reactions of others to different behaviours. The concept of equilibrium becomes less central. The ontological fundamentals of this central region involve institutional structures and algorithmic learning processes entailing program-like habits and rules (Hodgson 1997, 2007a, 2007c, Potts 2000, Vanberg 2004). As Kurt Dopfer *et al.* (2004, p. 263) put it: 'the central insight is that an economic system is a population of rules, a structure of rules, and a process of rules'. This conception makes explicit links between evolutionary economics and the study of institutions (Hodgson 2004, Hodgson and Stoelhorst 2014, Stoelhorst 2014).

Note how evolutionary and institutional economics occupy the centre of the diagram. The oddity is that mainstream economics has journeyed around the periphery rather than the centre of this domain. Evolutionary and institutional economics may thus have the potential to be a new mainstream (Hodgson 2007c).

This evolutionary-economics-as-mainstream outcome is resisted by the preference for complete analytical formalism in mainstream economics (Klamer and Colander 1990, Krueger 1991, Blaug 1997, 1999). But rather than designing models to reach complete analytical solutions, evolutionary economics often employs algorithmic approaches and techniques such as agent-based modelling. Besides employing 'formal' (principally mathematical) theory, evolutionary economists emphasise the additional importance and role of (more empirically driven and discursive) 'appreciative' theorising (Nelson and Winter 1982, p. 46).

Such a possible shift in the nature of mainstream economics was predicted by Frank Hahn (1991, pp. 48–50) when he wrote of putting aside 'the pleasures of theorems and proof' in favour of 'the uncertain embrace of history and sociology and biology'. Hahn also believed that 'the subject will return to its Marshallian affinities to biology'. Echoing such sentiments, Kenneth Arrow (1995, p. 1618) argued that 'the very notion of what constitutes an economic theory will have to change' and suggested that 'the biological is a more appropriate paradigm for economics than equilibrium models analogous to mechanics'.

But these statements by Arrow and Hahn are now decades old, and movement by mainstream economics in the direction they predicted has been relatively slow. Although there is increased discussion of the challenges of complex phenomena by mainstream economists and mechanisms of evolutionary selection are used in evolutionary game theory, the notions of equilibrium and optimization are still as prominent as they were in the 1980s and 1990s (Hodgson 2019, ch. 3).

4 Evolutionary Economics and Evolutionary Game Theory

This section compares evolutionary game theory with evolutionary economics. The review of evolutionary game theory here is brief and does not do justice to the enormous literature in this and related fields. Within game theory there are also other strains – such as behavioural game theory and cognitive game theory – that have interacted with evolutionary game theory. As well as embodying evolutionary concepts, much game theory now emphasises learning, which also may seem to resonate with evolutionary economics. But as shown below, evolutionary economics and game theory research are quite different in other respects.

Evolutionary game theory was first formally developed by Richard Lewontin (1961) in evolutionary biology. Subsequently Maynard Smith (1972, 1982, Maynard Smith and Price 1973) defined and developed the concept of an *evolutionarily stable strategy* (ESS). Robert Axelrod's (1984) use of game theory (involving selection among competing strategies) inspired many social scientists, and Robert Sugden (1986) imported the ESS concept into economics. Since the early 1990s there has been an explosion of interest in evolutionary games from economists and other social scientists.

There are important differences between classical games and evolutionary games. In many classical games, players have common knowledge about the rules and structure of the game, although this assumption is modified in behavioural game theory (Camerer 2003). But in all evolutionary games, players lack such common knowledge, have bounded rationality, and inherit rather than choose their strategies. Because players are selected from sizeable populations and matched randomly, they do not attempt to influence other players' future actions. This feature distinguishes evolutionary games from repeated games involving calculated strategic threats. At least in developments so far, players are relatively myopic and naïve in evolutionary games.

Evolutionary game theory claims significant success in modelling how social phenomena can arise from the interactions of utility-maximizing individuals. Examples include the emergence of altruism (Gintis 2003, Gintis *et al.* 2003, Nowak and Sigmund 2005, Sanchez and Cuesta 2005, Fletcher and Zwick 2007, Bowles and Gintis 2011), social learning (Kameda and Nakanishi 2003, Wakano *et al.* 2004, Wakano and Aoki 2006, Nakahashi 2007), social norms (Axelrod 1986, Binmore and Samuelson 1994, Ostrom 2000, Bicchieri 2006), moral behaviour (Skyrms 1996, 2004, Alexander 2007), and signalling and the emergence of language (Hurd 1995, Nowak *et al.* 1999, Zollman 2005, Pawlowitsch, 2007, 2008, Jäger 2008). Although some of the basic assumptions of these models are challengeable, the analytical significance of these contributions is widely acknowledged. It can be argued that many are useful heuristic models to help our understanding of reality on grounds similar to those proposed by Robert Sugden (2000). It has even been suggested that aspects of evolutionary game theory are redolent of the work of Veblen (Villena and Villena 2004).

Overall, evolutionary game theory has spawned a large and internally diverse set of approaches. But while evolutionary game theory now claims some empirical applications, the research field is not yet empirically driven to any great degree. It is propelled instead by formalistic explorations of the space of possible assumptions and by attempts to deal with problematic or incongruous formal outcomes or specifications. It reflects the norm in the prestigious core of mainstream economics itself and pays foremost attention to 'formal' rather than 'appreciative' theorising.

For Nelson and Winter (1982, pp. 45 ff.) a theory is 'a tool of inquiry'. The broad process of analysis and understanding – with a 'focus on the endeavour in which the theoretical tools are applied', including engagement with empirical data – amounts to *appreciative* theory. By contrast, with *formal* theory, 'the focus is on improving or extending or corroborating the tool itself'. For Nelson and Winter, these two different 'styles' or 'kinds' of theorising 'are necessary for economic understanding to progress satisfactorily, and there are strong if subtle connections between them'.

From a casual inspection of the two literatures of evolutionary economics and evolutionary game theory it is obvious that the former makes relatively more use of appreciative theorising, although both modes of argument can be found in either camp. While many evolutionary economists make use of formal models, the most well-known work in this field is more empirically orientated and empirically driven, as we show later.

A problem when comparing evolutionary game theory with evolutionary economics is that there is relatively little dialogue and overlap between the two genres. On the one hand, the 'formal' evolutionary game theorists rarely if ever refer to works by Dosi, Nelson, Winter, or Witt. They do not seem to regard their own game-theoretic work as a useful but optional tool to be used in the context of a broader process of theoretical enquiry into the nature of the world; rather it is often paraded and applauded as if it were sufficient theory itself. On the other hand, evolutionary economists make relatively little use of evolutionary or any other form of game theory, although some game-theoretic work has been published in *Journal of Evolutionary Economics*. Furthermore, when they turn to models, specifications of replicator dynamics are not placed in a game-theoretic context, and there are preferences for statistical approaches or agent-based modelling.

Agent-based models typically are applied to problems where the discovery of analytic solutions is difficult or impossible. But in such models, slight parametric or design changes often lead to very different simulation outcomes. As a result, many mainstream economists dismiss agent-based modelling, and it has limited exposure in the more prestigious journals of economics.

Matteo Richiardi and Roberto Leombruni (2005) pointed out that agent-based models are rare in twenty highly-rated journals in economics. They made up only 0.03 per cent of published articles in these journals since 1988. Richiardi and Leombruni reported common arguments against agent-based models – that they are often difficult to generalize, interpret, or estimate. The growth of agent-based models will be more significant for economics when they have achieved greater penetration into its top journals.

This leaves open the question of whether this failure of communication and cooperation between evolutionary economics and evolutionary game theory amounts to a lost opportunity. Is this failure principally a consequence of the divergent origins and initial purposes of the two modes of theorising? Consider the evolution of the two fields. Evolutionary economists rejected the enhanced rationality assumptions in mainstream economics in general and classical game theory in particular. The growth of modern evolutionary economics in the 1980s coincided with the turn to game theory by mainstream economics in the same decade (Rizvi 1994a, 1994b), but this was several years before the rise of evolutionary game theory. When it emerged, evolutionary game theory addressed quite different problems: it had the initial aim of solving equilibrium selection problems and dealing with multiple equilibria. But evolutionary economists eschewed optimization and simply accepted multiple equilibria without attempting to rank them. When evolutionary game theorists abandoned the hyper-rationality assumptions of classical game theory, they turned to models of human agents that were much less sophisticated than those already employed in evolutionary economics. The historical evolution of the two approaches did not encourage collaboration.

The purposes of the models employed by the two groups were also very different. While evolutionary game theorists tried to overcome problems of hyper-rationality and multiple equilibria in classical game theory, which in turn had taken over from general equilibrium theory when it developed internal problems (Rizvi 1994a), evolutionary economists focused on accepted empirical regularities and tried to show that their models, based on non-mainstream theoretical assumptions, could mimic these outcomes. Hence Nelson and Winter (1982) tried to replicate key facts concerning industrial structure and innovation, Gerald Silverberg *et al.* (1988) simulated the familiar S-shaped logistic curve of technological diffusion, and Giovanni Dosi *et al.* (1995) reproduced some important stylised facts of industrial dynamics and firm size distribution.

After the claimed success of these 'first-generation' models in evolutionary economics, attention shifted to more ambitious 'history-friendly' models that would not only replicate stylized facts but simulate the evolution of industrial patterns over a longer period of time (Malerba *et al.* 1999, Malerba and Orsenigo 2002). While the drive behind the development of evolutionary game theory was theoretical problems generated by previous formulations, evolutionary economics – while employing simulation models – has been more motivated to replicate and help explain observed empirical regularities in the industrial sphere.

Furthermore, and within limits, evolutionary economics has gradually broadened to overlap other genres, including the behavioural program in organizational analysis (Dosi *et al.* 2003). Partly as a result, computational modelling in evolutionary economics has become quite diverse and is no longer confined to models of the Nelson–Winter type.

But despite this diversity, it is fair to say that typical models in evolutionary economics are more empirically driven in their development than those in evolutionary game theory. This divergence between theoretically driven and empirically driven research agendas reflects a cultural and locational division within academia. University departments of economics, particularly in the English-speaking world, have become increasingly dominated by modes of theorising that are driven more by matters of mathematical technique than by engagement with empirical realities (Klamer and Colander 1990, Krueger 1991, Blaug 1997, 1999). By contrast, many evolutionary economists are located outside departments of economics, in business schools and elsewhere. These radical locational and cultural differences inhibit conversation and collaboration across different disciplines and locations. Perhaps research programmes addressing complexity and evolution would make more progress if they were located in bespoke interdisciplinary departments or institutes.

5 The 'Invisible College' of Evolutionary Thought

The future of a school of thought or stream of research does not depend simply on the attractiveness or explanatory power of its theory. Its ideas have prevailed within key organizations of academic power. The history of science shows repeatedly that today's accepted theories had to prevail over their inadequate predecessors by establishing communities and networks of followers.

By its very title, evolutionary economics pits itself against more static and equilibrium-oriented approaches that prevail in economics as a discipline. Yet success in changing economics has been limited. Furthermore, much work by self-described 'evolutionary economists' is now done outside departments of economics.

Juha-Antti Lamberg and I (Hodgson and Lamberg 2018) carried out a large-scale study of the state of 'evolutionary' thinking in business and economics.

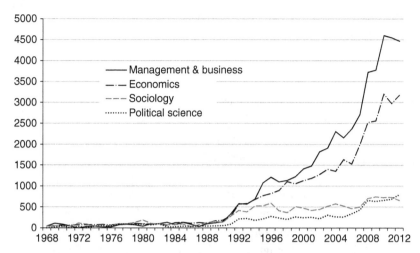

Figure 2 'Evolutionary' publications in management, economics, sociology, and politics

Number of publications in the Clarivate Analytics (formerly Thomson-Reuters) Web of Science with 'evolution' or derivative in the title, abstract, or keywords.

Figure 2 portrays the rapid rise since 1980 in research employing 'evolutionary' terminology. It reveals its particularly strong usage in management, business, and economics. This 'evolutionary' upsurge reflects the growing influence of the sets of ideas to which the term was attached. While not all uses of 'evolutionary' terminology can be described as 'evolutionary economics', the broader context is captured. Within the study, the supreme nodal significance of Nelson and Winter's (1982) work is clear.

An important institutional factor to take into account is the rapid growth of business schools after 1980, particularly in the USA but also elsewhere.[2] The co-citation analysis shows how the seminal and nodal work of Nelson and Winter (1982) has been linked most strongly to areas of business-related research. As discussed in the following section, its success is partly due to its implantation in business schools and other multidisciplinary milieux.

---

[2] In the USA, for example, the number of graduate degrees (masters and doctorates) conferred in business increased from 9.1 per cent of the total in 1970–71 to 21.2 per cent of the total in 2010–11 (National Center for Education Statistics 2017, Tables 323.10 and 324.10). In absolute terms, the number of such degrees increased almost sevenfold in the same period. *The Economist* (1996, p. 54) reported that 'the number of business schools in Britain has risen from 20 in the early 1980s to 120' by 1996. By 2012–13, 23.1 per cent of all postgraduate degrees in the UK were in business or administration (Higher Education Student Statistics UK 2018).

Hodgson and Lamberg's bibliometric analysis covered five five-year sub-periods, from 1986 to 2010. The following nomenclature was used to refer to clusters:

Cluster A   Industrial evolution and product life-cycles
Cluster B   National innovation systems
Cluster C   Economic sociology
Cluster D   Endogenous growth theory
Cluster E   Qualitative research methods
Cluster F   Socio-genetic evolution
Cluster G   Evolutionary game theory
Cluster H   Genetic algorithms (not shown in Figure 3)[3]
 Cluster I   Organizational ecology
 Cluster J   Evolution of technology and dominant designs
Cluster K   Resource and capability-based views
Cluster L   Organizational learning and behavioural approaches
Cluster M   New institutional sociology
Cluster N   Transaction cost economics

The clusters were formed via a bibliometric algorithm (see Hodgson and Lamberg 2018, Appendix). The choice of titles for the clusters was based on the nature of the key works that dominate each cluster, often using standard terminology. Note that relatively few of the clusters span established disciplinary boundaries. Clusters C, I, and M are largely, if not entirely confined to sociology. Clusters D and G are almost entirely, and Cluster N is largely, confined to economics. Other clusters relate to specialist groups of researchers with their own institutional niches in academia. So Clusters A and J relate to technology studies, Clusters I and L to organization science, and Cluster K to business strategy.

While in 1986–90 modern evolutionary approaches were just emerging, by 2006–10, the popularity of evolutionary views had increased considerably. Nelson and Winter (1982) stood near the centre of a heterogeneous constellation of clusters and research areas.

Over the period of analysis, management- and organization-related research streams had much gained in influence. Cluster G on evolutionary game theory, however, remained remote from the main streams of evolutionary research, with the exception of its links with Cluster F. Cluster N on transaction cost

---

[3] Cluster H appears in other figures in Hodgson and Lamberg (2018). The same lettering of clusters is preserved here as in the Hodgson and Lamberg paper for ease of cross-referencing.

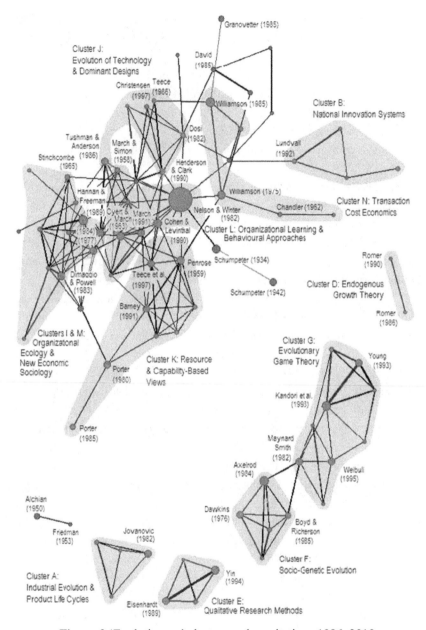

Figure 3 'Evolutionary' clusters and co-citations 1986–2010

economics (Coase 1937; Williamson 1975, 1985) endured on the fringes of the evolutionary research field.

The size of the node represents the relative citing frequency of the document. The thickness of the line connecting two documents indicates the strength of the link between the documents. Not all nodes are labelled in this version. This figure is a simplification of a more detailed version found in Hodgson and Lamberg (2018).

Figure 3 presents the structure of evolutionary research during the whole period of 1986–2010. The enduring nodal role of Nelson and Winter (1982) is impressive. There is a significant connection with Dosi's (1982) seminal essay on technological paradigms plus various works on organizational learning and behaviouralism (March and Simon 1958; Cohen and Levinthal 1990; March 1991).

Rather than creating an immediate cluster of closely related and spin-off research, the seminal role of Nelson and Winter (1982) has been to serve as a point of reference for other clusters. It seems that Nelson and Winter's work stimulated a dispersed array of related but detached enquiries but did not lead to the further development of a closely related and distinctive evolutionary theory in that genre (Witt 2008, Silva and Teixeira 2009).

In fact, a group of works on evolutionary theory in economics, including the famous papers by Armen Alchian (1950) and Milton Friedman (1953), did not meet the threshold level that we set for cluster status, and only these two papers met the threshold citation levels for appearance in Figure 3.

Overall, in 1986–2010 the work of Nelson and Winter (1982) was most closely linked with Cluster L on organizational learning and behavioural approaches, Cluster I on organizational ecology, Cluster M on new institutional sociology, and (more remotely) Cluster B on national innovation systems. Strikingly, this work is taught infrequently in departments of economics, and it is much more prominent in business schools. Further evidence of the detachment of Nelson–Winter-style evolutionary economics from its originating discipline is the absence of any significant interchange between evolutionary economics and evolutionary game theory (Hodgson and Huang 2012). There are links between Nelson and Winter (1982) and the work of Coase (1937) and Williamson (1975, 1985), but transaction cost economics has also moved its centre of gravity away from economics and towards business schools, as evidenced by a detailed longitudinal analysis of references in Williamson's work (Pessali 2006).

While Nelson and Winter's pioneering work remained relatively marginal in its source discipline of economics (particularly because of the increasing emphasis on mathematical theory in mainstream economics), it became very popular in management. Nelson and Winter (1982) became a central work for a while in clusters J and L; much of the research in these clusters is produced in business schools.

In the years 1983–9 inclusive, there were 142 citations to Nelson and Winter (1982) from journals listed under 'economics' in the Clarivate Analytics database, compared to eighty-two citations from journals in business and management. In 1990 the number of citations to this book from economics journals was equal to those from business and management journals. Subsequently citations from business and management journals increased rapidly, while the number of citations from economics journals grew much more slowly. In the years 2006–12 inclusive, there were 515 citations to this work from journals listed under 'economics' compared to 1,766 citations from journals in business and management.

In sum, in the 1980s the main arena for discussion of Nelson and Winter (1982) was in economics, but by 2006 citations to it from journals in business and management were more than three times greater than those from economics. As the evolutionary economics of Nelson and Winter (1982) has become more influential, it has become detached from mainstream economics while being cited much more in the business school sector.[4]

But the loss of a single home discipline has in turn created severe problems of unity and conversation across multiple clusters and research programs. Analyses of curricula in business schools have long noted limited success in linking separate disciplines, except for the use of common mathematical and statistical tools (Dunning 1989, Starkey and Madan 2001).

Both individual sub-periods and the years 1986–2010 overall provide strong evidence that the disciplinary boundary between economics and sociology has affected the linkages. In particular, work in Clusters I and M was not as close to Nelson and Winter's nodal work as it could be, despite the strong evolutionary theme to much work in organizational ecology (Hannan and Freeman 1989) and the work on the evolution of organizations by Aldrich (1999) and others.

All sub-periods show an enduring disconnection of research gathered around Nelson and Winter (1982) from evolutionary anthropology (Boyd and Richerson 1985), evolutionary psychology, work on the evolution of cooperation (Axelrod 1984), and Darwin (1859) himself. Given that the core theory of Nelson–Winter-style evolutionary economics may benefit from further

---

[4] But further evidence suggests an even deeper divergence. The three journals citing Nelson and Winter most often since 1983, which are listed under 'economics' in the Clarivate Analytics database, are *Industrial and Corporate Change* (accounting for 3.0 per cent of all citations to Nelson and Winter (1982)), *Journal of Evolutionary Economics* (2.6 per cent), and *Journal of Economic Behavior and Organization* (2.2 per cent): none of these is by any account a mainstream journal of economics. In the top ten, the seven other journals citing Nelson and Winter most since 1983 are *Research Policy* (5.7 per cent), *Strategic Management Journal* (5.7 per cent), *Organization Science* (3.7 per cent), *Management Science* (2.1 per cent), *International Journal of Technology Management* (1.9 per cent), and *Journal of Management Studies* (1.8 per cent).

development, these lively, theoretically rich, and relevant evolutionary literatures would be obvious places to turn for inspiration. So far, this has not
happened to any great degree.

While this analysis identifies Nelson and Winter (1982) as an enduring nodal
point in the evolution of the field, the bibliometric diagnosis suggests that this
work has not inspired major subsequent development of the core evolutionary
theory. Instead it serves as an historic 'concept marker' (Case and Higgins
2000) with 'conceptual symbolism' (Small 2004, p. 71) for a diverse,
interdisciplinary, and fragmented field of specialized 'evolutionary' studies of
particular economic and business phenomena. This also suggests that this
'evolutionary' field lacks an integrated, developing meta-theoretical perspective, which can help to generate shared ideas and research questions for
empirical investigation.

6 Problems of Identity and Strategy

Any viable discipline or school of thought must have a *raison d'être*. This can
be defined in terms of

(a) the study of a specific zone of enquiry or a set of phenomena in the real
world,
(b) the promotion or development of a particular theoretical approach (such as
utility maximization or the use of evolutionary theory),
(c) the promotion or development of a set of analytical techniques (such as
econometrics, game theory, or agent-based models), or
(d) the promotion or development of policies in a defining problem area (such
as the environment, peace, or economic development).

The *raison d'être* may consist of one of these or a combination of more than one.

Starting with the first option, evolutionary economics has not made a major
effort to define itself in terms of (a) – a specific zone of enquiry or a set of
phenomena in the real world. While the field has emphasized innovation and
technological change, this is because they are often sidelined in mainstream
theory – not because this zone of enquiry is regarded as sufficient to define the
essence of evolutionary economics. Indeed the term 'evolutionary economics'
has been promoted by protagonists in diverse contexts other than innovation and
technological change.

Turning to (d), although Nelson–Winter-type evolutionary economics has
made important policy contributions, particularly in regard to science and
technology, contributions to policy development do not themselves define
'evolutionary economics'. Hence (d) alone does not provide a *raison d'être,*
even if the field has been a major area of contribution.

This leaves us with (b) or (c) as potential *raisons d'être* for evolutionary economics. Different opinions may exist on this. A core theoretical approach is evident in Nelson and Winter (1982). On the other hand, some evolutionary economists have adopted and promoted specific techniques, such as Stuart Kauffman's (1995) NK model and agent-based modelling. But in neither case does our bibliometric evidence point to extensive post-1982 development of these theories or techniques. Whatever the *raison d'être* of evolutionary economics, the Hodgson–Lamberg bibliometric analysis fails to detect its defining developmental traces in post-1982 publications.

This does not mean that there have been no core theoretical developments in this field since 1982. Some are cited in this essay. But none of these have established strong bibliometric traces in the citation record. Unfortunately, no development has yet created strong and enduring resonance.

The complete explanation of this lacuna would require a major research project, beyond the scope of this Element. Consider one possible reason among others. We hypothesize that the migration of evolutionary economics from departments of economics to business schools and other multidisciplinary institutes has exacerbated its ongoing fragmentation and thwarted the development of its identity, at least in terms of theory or technique ((b) or (c)). This migration also created great opportunities, particularly on the policy front. But policy influence may have relieved survival pressure and helped to postpone the development of a core theoretical identity.

Success in these interdisciplinary milieux has been a major blessing but also in part a curse. Like oil-rich countries enjoying prosperity but failing to invest revenues in long-lasting and productive assets such as infrastructure and education, evolutionary economics has failed to invest in a viable theoretical core or provide another suitable *raison d'être*. Well over thirty years since the publication of Nelson and Winter (1982), and without adequate further theoretical development or other reinvigoration, there are diminishing marginal returns in an inexorably fragmented and specialist field.

Science is a social process and it works partly through the creation and ongoing amendment of established positions in a scientific community (Kuhn 1962, Polanyi 1962, Kitcher 1993). Its social practices establish 'epistemic communities' and institutionalized 'machineries of knowing' (Knorr-Cetina 1981). Sufficient variety of opinion in any scientific community is necessary for advance so that inadequate or flawed beliefs can be challenged by alternatives. Variety and contestation are essential for progress.

Some sufficient (but not absolute) consensus is also required to avoid endless criticism and unceasing demolition of core beliefs (Polanyi 1962,

Kitcher 1993). It is impossible for individual scientists to challenge everything effectively. There are far too many theories and publications. Many things have to be taken on trust. Judgments of others have to be relied upon, often without detailed inspection. Lots of things have to be taken for granted by individual scholars; otherwise, everyone would be engaged in verifying or challenging everything, and science would not make any progress.

But consensus has difficulties in academic communities that are also trained and required to be sceptical and critical. To the extent that some consensus is necessary, it requires incentives to be sustained (Kitcher 1993). The leaders in the scientific community must have sufficient power over career opportunities, academic promotions, academic journals, and grant-awarding bodies to provide reputational, pecuniary, and other rewards for individuals to respect many existing scientific claims, and not to be overly critical of its consensus.

The obvious danger here is that the group becomes overly conservative, rebuts much sensible criticism, and stifles innovation. This has happened in some disciplines. But the complete absence of consensus would also be damaging: endless criticism and unrestrained innovation would inhibit cumulative advance in the healthiest areas of research. Hence, to a degree, institutionalized incentives for maintaining some consensus matter.

The Nelson–Winter wave of evolutionary economics established some conversational forums and consensus-preserving institutions. These include the International Joseph Schumpeter Society formed in 1986. There are allied or sympathetic journals such as *Journal of Evolutionary Economics* and *Industrial and Corporate Change*. These provided important, international, consensus-preserving incentives and helped to keep evolutionary economics together, especially on a global scale.

But otherwise, and within particular universities, reputational and other incentives have been underdeveloped. Having failed to capture major citadels of mainstream economics, evolutionary economics took hold in other, multidisciplinary environments. Here goals and incentives are more diverse, emanating from multiple disciplines. In such contexts, most evolutionary economists have to advance their individual careers in compartmentalized research fields such as innovation studies, business economics, science policy, or organization studies. It is understandable and possibly justifiable that no one has attempted to set up academic departments labelled 'evolutionary economics' with their own qualifications and teaching programs. But this has left evolutionary economics in fragmented environments, where plural incentives and overlapping structures were less aligned to its mission or interests.

As it moved into business schools and other interdisciplinary institutions, evolutionary economics faced the crucial additional problem of establishing interdisciplinary mechanisms to generate fruitful conversation and sustain sufficient scientific consensus. But the necessary degree of consensus is more difficult to sustain in such contexts. Researchers have vested interests and incentives – including those of promotion, status, and publication – that are largely compartmentalized by the institutional and departmental structures of academia (Weingart and Stehr 2000). Specialisation within disciplines compounds this problem further. Any interdisciplinary research program has to provide additional incentives – including common questions of interest – to escape multiple, narrow, specialist confinements.

Put in this context, the success of evolutionary economics in maintaining fruitful conversation among its practitioners has been very much against the stream. It is due to the enduring vitality of several international networks (including the International Schumpeter Society and allied journals) and some national associations. But the bibliometric evidence in Hodgson and Lamberg (2018) reveals insufficient further development of a theoretical core. Studies of academic activity from the sociology of science suggest that additional institutionalized incentives are necessary.

Hodgson and Lamberg (2018) charted the diversification and spectacular growth of 'evolutionary' research from 1986 to 2010. Their study reveals a combination of growth, diversification, and deepening fragmentation, caused in large part by disciplinary boundaries that cannot be dissolved simply by the use of vague words such as 'evolution', 'evolutionary', or 'selection'.

This diverse 'invisible college' of 'evolutionary' research has striking differences from 'invisible colleges' studied elsewhere. Classically the term applied to 'an elite of mutually interacting and productive scientists within a research area' (Crane 1972, p. 348). Although the 'evolutionary' field in economics, sociology, and management has an elite group of highly cited researchers, their works are also divided by disciplinary and sub-disciplinary frontiers. The identity and boundaries of its research area are unclear. It is a peculiarly diverse and segmented elite, making relatively few shared references to core theoretical works appearing after 1982.

Consequently, 'evolutionary' work in economics, sociology, and business has not generated enduring, transdisciplinary questions for successful empirical or theoretical research. In this diverse context, the narrower stream of evolutionary economics lacks an adequate theoretical 'hard core' in the sense of Imré Lakatos (1970). Hodgson and Lamberg's (2018) bibliometric analysis clearly establishes the work of Nelson and Winter (1982) as a dominant node in economics, management, and business, but there is a lack of subsequent identifiable literature developing a core theoretical framework. Its enduring presence among the citations in the field seems as much a ceremonial and 'symbolic payment of intellectual debts' (Small 2004, p. 71) as anything else.

Each individual cluster in the field manifests a high degree of historical path dependence and a good measure of isolation. Path dependence is itself susceptible to bibliometric study (Lucio-Arias and Leydesdorff 2008). The silo effect (Lewin and Volberda 1999) refers to an outcome of specialization and fragmentation where subfields become less capable of reciprocal operation with other related subfields. The evidence in Hodgson and Lamberg (2018) suggests that evolutionary economics may be moving dangerously in this direction.

Consequently, if evolutionary economics is to develop in the future it needs to find ways to (1) further facilitate inter-cluster communication, (2) promote complementary integration between clusters, and (3) generate prominent research questions with potential answers that are superior to those produced by rival approaches.

It is a longstanding claim that much innovation in science comes from the synthesis of ideas from different topics or disciplines (Peirce [1882] 1958, Koestler 1964, Laudan 1977). But as noted above, scientific innovation requires not only diversity but also a sufficiency of consensus and community, with a shared conceptual language, to make such synergy possible. Some consensus is also necessary to avoid continually overturning every established assumption or result (Polanyi 1962, Kitcher 1993).

One of the key problems is fragmentation and specialization. All scientific fields face the unrelenting challenge of what Eli Noam (1995, p. 248) calls the 'inexorable specialization of scholars' as research digs deeper and deeper into specific, separate problems (Blau 1994, Wenger 1998). Within the field of evolutionary economics, fragmentation and specialization have not been matched by fruitful development of overarching theory, a common conceptual vocabulary, and common research questions promising answers that demonstrate the superiority of the approach.

Communication is inhibited by insufficient shared terminology. Organizational ecologists use some specialized vocabulary that differs from that of evolutionary economists. There is also the lack of a shared overarching 'evolutionary' theoretical framework. Words such as 'evolution', 'co-evolution', 'evolutionary', or 'selection' are used in very different ways, with grossly insufficient attempts to establish shared meanings (Hodgson 2013a, Dollimore and Hodgson 2014, Hodgson and Stoelhorst 2014).

Consider, for example, the literature on 'co-evolution' in organization science. This refers loosely to developmental interaction between organizations and their environments. But the word 'evolution' in this literature is often taken for granted. For example, the editors (Lewin and Koza 2001) of an entire issue of *Organization Studies* devoted to 'co-evolution' referred to 'the co-evolution framework', 'the co-evolution perspective', 'the co-evolution construct', and 'evolutionary theory' (singular) with little further explanation. It is unclear whether 'evolution' referred to a single entity or a population of entities. The authors usefully mentioned the conceptual triplet of 'variation, selection, and retention' but again with no further explanation. What we were not told is what *selection* means and *what* is being *retained*. (These issues may appear to be simple, but they are not.) The origins of that conceptual triplet were uncited, and we were not reminded that this triplet refers to the conceptual core of Darwinism. As elsewhere, there was a remarkable reluctance to mention Darwin. There was also no mention of the fact that Darwin's evolutionary framework is very different from others, such as that of Lamarck or Spencer. Considerable vagueness and imprecision is perpetuated.[5]

In the 'evolutionary' literature there is some mention of 'selection' but rarely an elaboration of its precise meaning and Darwinian context. For example, J. Peter Murmann *et al.* (2003) gave a reflection for the new millennium on the state and future of 'evolutionary' research in management and organization theory. Their article illustrates the problems as well as the potentialities. Its authors mentioned the concept of 'selection' many times but failed to give it a sufficiently clear meaning. There was little elaboration of what exactly is being selected, what the selection mechanisms are, and what kind of population-level outcomes of selection need to be identified. While the authors rightly stressed the importance of empirical work, the key concepts to be deployed for analysing reality remained vague. Immersion in empirics alone cannot serve as a research program, especially if it is conceptually blind.

An obvious longstanding candidate for a shared theoretical evolutionary framework, deploying sharper meanings of these terms, is the generalization of Darwinian principles to the socio-economic domain (Veblen 1898, 1899, Campbell 1965, Hull 1988, Hodgson and Knudsen 2010). But work in this area has had little presence within Nelson–Winter-type evolutionary economics until recently, and it

---

[5] Lewin and Volberda (1999, p. 523) and Lewin and Koza (2001, p. v) included Max Weber and Alfred Chandler as exponents of 'evolutionary theory', and Lewin and Koza did so in the same paragraph in which they briefly mentioned 'variation, selection, and retention'. In fact, neither Weber nor Chandler made much of this conceptual triplet. We were not informed that the 'variation, selection, and retention' formulation is particularly associated with a classic essay by Donald T. Campbell (1965) which explicitly described these concepts as Darwinian and pioneered their application to social evolution.

is far from universally accepted (Aldrich *et al.* 2008; Stoelhorst 2008, 2014; Hodgson and Knudsen 2010; Breslin 2011; Hodgson and Stoelhorst 2014).

Without such integrative developments, evolutionary economics is likely to suffer further fragmentation, albeit with innovation and progress within the individual fragments. A core theoretical framework is necessary to show that the approach has improved answers to pressing research questions to claim its superiority over rival approaches.

Some links have yet to be developed between evolutionary economics and other streams of evolutionary research. While evolutionary economists, organizational ecologists, and institutional economists have often distanced themselves from narrow versions of rationality and have been influenced by behaviouralists such as Simon (1957), much less attention has been given to evolutionary psychology (Cosmides and Tooby 1994a, 1994b, Buss 1999) and the evolution of cooperation (Hammerstein 2003, Bowles and Gintis 2011). The missing links with earlier classic works in this area such as Axelrod (1984) and Boyd and Richerson (1985) are clearly evident from the Hodgson–Lamberg bibliometric analysis.

All this suggests that evolutionary economics needs a much clearer identity and *raison d'être*. Bibliometric analysis identifies the failure to develop a prominent and widely cited theoretical core. This is not to belittle the many achievements of evolutionary economics but to point to enduring gaps that need to be addressed in the future.

7 Back to Ontological Basics

Despite the variety of approaches involved, it is possible to find some shared concerns at a basic level. The most fundamental issues are ontological. They address the nature of the world to which the principles of evolutionary economics are said to apply. We find that among contemporary evolutionary economists there is universal agreement on five important features.

First, it is a world of change. But this change is not merely quantitative or parametric: it involves qualitative changes in technology, organisations, and the structure of the economy (Veblen 1919, Schumpeter 1934, Hayek 1988). The equilibrium orientation of much mainstream economics is criticised precisely for its limited ability to embrace such qualitative change (Klaes 2004). In its emphasis on process rather than equilibrium, evolutionary economics aspires to characterize transient effects even in the presence of a well-defined rest point in the long-term dynamics. Attention to dynamics is one of the common hallmarks of all strands of thinking described as 'evolutionary'.

Second, an important feature of economic change is the generation of novelty. What are the sources of innovation and change? Variety and its replenishment through novelty and creativity is a central theme of contemporary evolutionary economics. Nicolai Foss (1994, p. 21) argued that evolutionary economics of the type developed by Giovanni Dosi, Richard Nelson, Sidney Winter, Ulrich Witt, and others is concerned with 'the transformation of already existing structures and the emergence and possible spread of novelties'. Witt (1992, p. 3) wrote: 'for a proper notion of socioeconomic evolution, an appreciation of the crucial role of novelty, its emergence, and its dissemination, is indispensable'.

Third, evolutionary economists stress the complexity of economic systems. There are various definitions of ontological complexity, but many invoke the key idea of causal interaction between entities with varied characteristics (Saviotti 1996). Such complex ontologies involve nonlinear and potentially chaotic interactions, further limiting predictability. They create the possibility of emergent properties and further novelties; and generally the combination of novelty and complexity makes many evolutionary changes irreversible (Dosi and Metcalfe 1991).

Fourth, human agents have limited cognitive capacities. Especially given the complexity, uncertainty, and ongoing change in the real world, agents are unable to fully understand what is going on or what is likely to happen. They are unable to obtain a fully specified set of options and decisions based on simpler rules of thumb rather than comprehensive rational deliberation. As Herbert Simon (1957) put it, there is 'bounded rationality'. Unlike much of mainstream economics until recently, agents are not assumed to act as if they were capable of solving complex optimization problems with large amounts of data.

Fifth, complex phenomena can emerge through self-organisation or piece-meal iteration rather than comprehensive overall design. Just as Darwin showed that intricate and complex phenomena can emerge without God, evolutionary economists adopt the insight of Friedrich Hayek (1988) and others that many human institutions and other social arrangements evolve spontaneously through individual interactions, without an overall planner or blueprint. In both natural and social evolution, much is the outcome of spontaneous ordering and not deliberate design.

These five features are widely if not universally accepted among evolutionary economists. But beyond this point some divergences begin.

For example, universal acceptance of the importance of self-organisation or undesigned order does not mean unanimity on its ontological details or its explanatory significance. One crucial problem is whether markets or exchange are the universal ether of human interaction (from which spontaneous order emerges) or whether markets and contracts depend significantly on other institutions (such as the state – whose evolution in turn has to be explained), which may in fact involve a significant measure of planning or design as well as spontaneity (Vanberg 1986, Hodgson 1993, 2009). Differences of view over the latter issue lead to a variety of policy positions over the roles of states or markets in the evolutionary college.

There is also a divergence over whether the idea of self-organisation is sufficient to explain social evolution (Foster 1997, p. 444), or it is an 'abstract, general description of evolutionary processes' (Witt 1997, p. 489), or it has to be supplemented by other major mechanisms including selection (Kauffman 1993, Hodgson and Knudsen 2006, 2010, Aldrich *et al.* 2008, Geisendorf 2009). This latter divergence relates to a fundamental difference in ontological assumptions. Does the 'evolutionary' analysis relate to the 'evolution' (or development) of a *single* entity, or does it address the 'evolution' of a whole *population* of entities. Confusion or conflation of these different types of 'evolution' has often created unwarranted controversy and copious misunderstanding.

In modern biology the former aspect (one-entity 'evolution') is typically referred to as development or ontogeny, and the latter (the 'evolution' of a population) as evolution or phylogeny. Accordingly, we may make the distinction between:

a) *ontogenetic or developmental theories of social evolution* that focus princi-pally on a single entity or structure and consider its development through time; and

b) *phylogenetic or population theories of social evolution* that address the evolution of whole populations of entities, as well as the development of entities themselves.

For example, Hegel's and Marx's theories of history fall in the category of ontogenetic or developmental theories of social evolution. In *Capital* Marx (1976, pp. 90–2) focused on capitalism's development as largely a result of its own internal logic. Spencer defined evolution in terms of a single system and the development of its internal complexity. Schumpeter was strongly influenced by Marx and focused principally on the development of singular systems. Like Marx, he saw evolution as the development of a single system, largely 'from within' (Schumpeter, 1934, p. 63). Witt (2003) similarly emphasized endogenous change.

Evolution 'from within' downplays interactions with the environment. It either concentrates on a single entity or defines the system so broadly that everything of interest is 'within'. Either way, the focus is on a singular entity or system rather than a population of entities. But there is always an external environment. History shows that many social, economic, or political changes result from exogenous shocks. Developments 'from within' are also vitally important, but it is a mistake to give them exclusive stress. In biology, neither individuals, nor species, nor ecosystems are entirely 'self-transforming'. Evolution takes place within *open* systems involving *both* endogenous and exogenously stimulated change.

In social evolution, exogenously stimulated change is sometimes of great importance, partly because of the cultural mechanisms of imitation and conformism that tend to reduce internal variety and can lead to institutional ossification. Exogenous shocks sometimes overcome the rigidity of social systems. In history there are many examples of the role of exogenous shocks.

The arrival of American warships in Tokyo Bay led to the Meiji Restoration of 1868 and the abrupt transition of Japan from feudalism to a Western-inspired capitalist society. The occupation of Japan and Germany by American and allied troops in 1945 also led to major institutional changes. The course of institutional evolution was altered by the intrusion of new forces across the boundaries of the system, as in many other cases of institutional transformation being promoted by invasion or other forces from outside.

Ontogenetic approaches themselves put different degrees of emphasis on the role of environmental interactions. In some accounts ontogeny is treated as the 'unrolling' of the phenomenon with an outcome that is predestined and independent of environmental contingencies. More realistically, ontogeny involves sequential adaptation to environmental circumstances and events. But in both cases a singular entity is involved.

Self-organization is insufficient to deal with cases of multiple entities. It provides no adequate explanation of how one entity rather than another adapts to survive in this environment. On its own, self-organization theory can explain neither current adaptedness nor the process of adaptation to the environment (Cziko 1995, p. 323). Self-organization is important in nature and society, but it cannot offer a complete explanation of evolution in populations.

In contrast, phylogenetic or population theories of social evolution enlarge the scope of evolutionary theory from one entity to a population of entities and introduce a number of additional critical issues. First, there is the existence and possible regeneration of variety among this population. Second, there is the question of the differential survival of different members. As a result of accident, choice, or differential fitness, some survive longer than others. Third, there is the possibility that some members of the population may pass on information concerning population solutions to others.

We are reminded of Darwin's (1859) famous trinity of principles of variation, selection, and inheritance. Darwinian ideas, however, have been strongly resisted in the social sciences for most of the twentieth century (Degler 1991). We return to the question of Darwinism later.

The contrast between ontogenetic and phylogenetic theories of evolution stems from differences in the types of phenomena being addressed: ontogenetic theories address singular developing entities, including social formations such as institutions, while phylogenetic theories address populations, with an interest in the differential survival capacities of different entities. Matters are more complicated because phylogenetic evolution always also involves the ontogenetic development of individual entities. Furthermore, ontogenetic development may involve phylogenetic selection of components, such as the selection of bacteria in the guts of animals, or the selection of teams within firms.

As noted above, Menger's (1871) theory of the evolution of money is an example of an ontogenetic theory. Although it involves multiple individual traders, the focus is not on their differential survival but on the emergence of money as an institution. But when Veblen (1899, p. 188) wrote of 'the natural selection of institutions' he was concerned with their differential survival as well as the natural selection of individuals.

Further taxonomic divisions arise when we consider what populations of entities are relevant in the social domain. Several early theorists of phylogenetic social evolution regarded either human individuals or ideas as the appropriate entities or units (Hodgson 2004a, ch. 5). But the choice of individuals as units of selection has accommodated a number of views concerning human nature, including the extreme view that it is wholly and biologically determined. A key question is this: what makes an entity social, rather than merely being a common attribute of a number of individuals? An adequate answer to this question must point to social structures or relations that are irreducible to the properties of individuals taken severally. This suggests that an exclusive focus on individuals as units of selection in social evolution is inadequate.

In this respect the lead offered by Nelson and Winter (1982) is particularly important. Using the analogy of 'routines as genes', they argued that organisational routines involving groups of workers act as replicators in the evolution of firms. Although this insight has led to a new way of viewing firms and their evolution, the details remain controversial, and many writers have stressed the need to define the replicator concept more carefully (Hodgson and Knudsen 2010). Nevertheless, the idea of 'routines as genes' signals that routines are replicators in the social and organizational domain, analogous to genes as replicators in the biological world.

Further differences of view arise over basic questions concerning 'what evolves' in the so-called 'evolutionary' process. Different theoretical approaches tend to focus on different basic units as well as different mechanisms of change. One of the arguments for the adoption of a core set of 'evolutionary' principles is that it would help answer key questions concerning the units and mechanisms of evolution.

8 The Need for General Principles

In this section we address the evolution of populations of entities that have differential capacities for survival and can replicate key information to pass from one to another. These may be described as 'complex population systems' (Hodgson and Knudsen 2010). There are examples of these broadly defined systems in both nature and human society. Accordingly, some leading evolutionary economists have advanced the idea that general, overarching evolutionary principles may apply to both biological and social evolution. Sidney Winter (1987, p. 617) argued that

> natural selection and evolution should not be viewed as concepts developed for the specific purposes of biology and possibly appropriable for the specific purposes of economics, but rather as elements of the framework of a new conceptual structure that biology, economics and other social sciences can comfortably share.

Similarly, J. Stanley Metcalfe (1998, pp. 21–2, 36) proposed that a common set of 'evolutionary ideas' apply to both social and biological phenomena: 'Evolutionary theory is a manner of reasoning in its own right quite independently of the use made of it by biologists. They simply got there first '. But while upholding abstract principles that span both the biological and the social domains, Winter and Metcalfe refrained from describing them as Darwinian.

An objection to such generalisations is that the processes of biological and socio-cultural evolution are so different that the generalization of Darwinian or other principles to encompass them is unhelpful (Cordes 2006). There are problems, however, with the argument that biological and social evolution are so different that any general principles are unviable. First, it overlooks the fact that detailed mechanisms of evolution also differ greatly *within* the biological world. These differences of mechanism are as impressive in some ways as the differences between the biological and the social. Yet general (Darwinian) principles still apply. As David Hull (1988, p. 403) argued: 'the amount of increased generality needed to accommodate the full range of biological phenomena turns out to be extensive enough to include social and conceptual evolution as well'.

Generalization is central to all science, which compares and groups varied phenomena for the purpose of explanation. It is obvious, even trivial, that such generalisation covers diverse phenomena and cannot capture all the details. Generalizations operate at a higher level of abstraction, and this does not mean that we ignore the details and particularities at a lower level. We all know that the mechanisms of biological and social evolution are very different. Generalized Darwinism neither neglects nor overturns this truth.

Darwinism has revolutionized our understanding of the natural world, but it has had a limited impact in the social sciences (Degler 1991). Nevertheless, since 1990 there has been increasing interest in Darwinism in the social sciences, in terms of helping to explain underlying human dispositions and providing general abstract principles to frame our investigations into evolutionary processes in society. Arguably, general Darwinian principles apply to both biological and social evolution at a highly abstract level (Hodgson and Knudsen 2006, 2010, Aldrich *et al.* 2008). Indeed, no other viable set of general evolutionary principles has been discovered for populations of replicating entities.

But a host of misunderstandings surround these ventures. Contrary to widespread belief, Darwinian scientific principles do not support any form of racism, sexism, nationalism, or imperialism. Darwinism does not imply that militant conflict is inevitable, that human inequalities or power or wealth are unavoidable, that cooperation or altruism are unimportant or unnatural, that evolution always leads to optimization or progress, that social phenomena can or should be explained in terms of biology alone, that organisms can or should be explained in terms of their genes alone, that human intention is unimportant, or that human agency is blind or mechanistic.

Importantly, humans differ from plants and most animals in that we have language and culture. We prefigure many actions and consequences in our minds and act intentionally. While studying socio-economic evolution we are concerned with human welfare and well-being, and not merely with survival or fecundity. The paces and timescales of social and biological evolution are typically very different. All this is vitally important, but it does not diminish the analytical value of Darwinism in general, overarching terms in the social domain.

Darwinism upholds the notion of *causal explanation* (where a cause is understood as necessarily involving transfers of matter or energy) as a basic tenet. Divine, spiritual, miraculous, or uncaused causes are ruled out. Generally, causal explanations invoke scientific principles or laws. Evolutionary explanations are in terms of connected causal sequences. Darwinism maintains that every event or phenomenon has a cause (Veblen 1898, Dennett 1995, Hodgson 2004b).

This principle applies to human intentionality as well as everything else. Contrary to widespread belief, causal explanation does not mean that intentions are ignored in Darwinism; it simply means that they are caused, and at some stage they need to be explained. The idea that every event has a cause implies neither that every event is predictable from its antecedents nor that the universe is a predictable machine. Is the idea that every event has a cause 'determinism'? Although it is widely used as a term of abuse, 'determinism' is an ambiguous and ill-defined word (Bunge 1959, Hodgson 2004a, pp. 58–62). The notion that every event has a cause is better described as the *principle of determinacy*. This principle is central to all science, and even to quantum physics, where causality is probabilistic.

The importance and enduring value of Darwinism lie in its elaboration of causal mechanisms of evolution with the entwined triple concepts of variation, inheritance, and selection. Darwinian evolution applies to populations of entities that face scarce resources and other difficulties and can pass on adaptive solutions to these problems to their successors. In principle, these mechanisms apply to any open and evolving system with a variety of units. Darwinian evolution occurs when there is some replicating entity that gives rise to imperfect copies of itself, and these copies do not have equal potential to survive.

Modern Darwinian theory makes a distinction between *replicators* and *interactors* (Hull 1988). Darwin hinted at a similar distinction but did not use this terminology. All *interactors* host one or more replicators. An *interactor* is a relatively cohesive entity, in a population of other similar interactors, which interacts with its environment and leads to differential replication. A *replicator* is hosted by an interactor, and it is best defined as an informational mechanism that can help guide or instruct the interactor. Particular kinds of replicator carry some additional information on how an interactor may develop and reproduce (Hodgson and Knudsen 2010, pp. 24, 76–88, 106–9, 112–150).[6]

While genes are one form of replicator in the biological domain, multiple candidate replicators exist in the socio-economic world, including habits, customs, and routines. These can operate simultaneously on multiple levels (Hodgson and Knudsen 2010).

In a Darwinian evolutionary process the interactors are the *objects* of selection. They face resources that are immediately scarce. Some survive or reproduce better than others. This leads to changes in the pool of replicator

---

[6] There is some criticism of the replicator concept in the literature. For example, Godfrey-Smith (2009, p. 5) misleadingly treats a replicator as an entity 'that makes copies of itself'. Instead, in our view, the replicator is an information-retaining and copiable mechanism, hosted by an interactor. Treating the replicator as an informational mechanism associated with an interactor dispenses with some of the problems identified by Godfrey-Smith and others. See Hodgson and Knudsen (2010, ch. 6) for responses to other criticisms of the replicator concept.

characteristics in the population as a whole. Hence changes in the replicator pool are *outcomes* of selection. Vague talk of 'units of selection' overlooks this key difference and often leads to confusion.

Another enduring confusion needs to be laid to rest. While Nelson and Winter (1982) invoked the Darwinian principles of variation, inheritance, and selection in their analysis, they refrained from describing them as Darwinian. Instead they labelled their approach as 'Lamarckism'. Lamarckism refers to the assumption that the characteristics developed by an entity (such as the tall neck of a giraffe) will be inherited by its progeny. This 'inheritance of acquired characters' is often (but not entirely) ruled out in the biological world, but often (typically without precise explanation) assumed to apply to evolution in the social world.

Nelson and Winter unwittingly reinforced the widespread assumption that Lamarckism and Darwinism are rivalrous and mutually exclusive. This false dichotomy endures in organisation studies and elsewhere (Usher and Evans 1996). For instance, the seminal work of Michael Hannan and John Freeman (1989) is described by many as 'Darwinian' because it stresses selection in a relatively static, industry-level environment and gives a low estimate for the possibilities of individual organizational adaptation. By contrast, those who give more stress to adaptation are described as Lamarckian.

This dichotomy is factually ungrounded and theoretically confused. It suggests that Darwin said nothing about development and adaptation. This is clearly wrong (Mayr 1991). In addition, Darwin himself believed that the inheritance of acquired characters was possible. In that sense, Darwin was a Lamarckian! Later many (Darwinian) biologists turned against the idea of Lamarckian inheritance. But logically, and in principle, Darwinism and Lamarckism are not mutually exclusive, contrary to many suggestions in the literature. The existence or nonexistence of Lamarckian inheritance is partly an empirical issue.

There is a fundamental theoretical problem with the Darwinism–Lamarckism dichotomy. Some acquired characters, such as ageing and injuries, are not beneficial; but for species to evolve, the effects of deleterious acquired characters must be restricted. Accordingly, Lamarckism *depends on* the Darwinian principle of selection in order to explain why any propensity to inherit acquired impairments does not prevail. As Richard Dawkins (1986, p. 300) argued, 'the Lamarckian theory can explain adaptive improvement in evolution only by, as it were, riding on the back of the Darwinian theory'. Lamarckism, if valid in any particular domain, depends on Darwinian mechanisms of selection for evolutionary guidance. If Lamarckism is valid, then it must be complemented by Darwinian selection.

Consequently, the core Darwinian principles are more general, and Lamarckian inheritance is a contingent option. When considering (say) the evolution of a population of business firms, it is an empirical matter whether forces of selection (such as through insolvency or bankruptcy) are stronger than forces of adaptation that help survival. Studies find evidence of both forces at work (Hodgson *et al.* 2017).

It is ironic that some authors claim that socio-economic evolution is Lamarckian, but not Darwinian, as if they were dichotomous. The irony exists because the very idea of Lamarckian inheritance relies on something like the (post-Darwinian) distinction between replicators and interactors. Why? Inheritance must mean something more than 'passed on' from one entity to another. Otherwise, dogs catching fleas or people being infected by a virus would be cases of inheritance. An example of Lamarckian 'inheritance' would be a child catching a cold from its mother. This would be nonsensical.

Clearly this is not what is normally meant by Lamarckian inheritance, and the idea of inheritance has to be more restrictive. It has to be confined to processes involving replicators. Lamarckism implies that the activity or development of an interactor somehow changes the information in its replicators, and this changed information is somehow passed on to its offspring. We need something like the replicator–interactor distinction to make sense of Lamarckism, even before we examine its veracity. Those that think otherwise are challenged to provide a definition of Lamarckism that uses the concept of inheritance in a sense that excludes contagion.

The idea of generalizing Darwinism to cover social entities has existed since Darwin's *Origin of Species*. But thanks to developments in the philosophy of biology and elsewhere it has recently been possible to give sufficient precision to its key concepts in generalized form (Price 1970, 1995, Hull 1988, Sterelny *et al.* 1996, Sperber 2000, Hodgson and Knudsen 2010). The challenge is to show that generalized Darwinism can have an important impact on the development of middle-range theory and serve as a useful guide for empirical enquiry.

Consider some questions to which generalized Darwinism may help to give answers. It is notable that the overall complexity of human society has increased dramatically – despite setbacks after the collapse of some civilisations – over the last few thousand years. By contrast, the emergence of complex organisms in nature has taken many millions of years. How can evolutionary economics begin to explain this discrepancy? The framework of generalized Darwinism offers a fruitful line of enquiry (Hodgson and Knudsen 2010). First, it addresses the general question of how the potential for complexity evolves in population systems.

A key theoretical result from this enquiry is that the faithful copying of information held in replicators is a necessary condition for the enlargement of the potential for complexity. As long as a system accurately retains its problem solutions it can build up this experience and test variations through a process of selection (Nelson 2008). If such vital information is lost or corrupted, then it has constantly to be rediscovered. This does not itself explain why human social complexity has evolved at a greater rate, but it does suggest that more developed societies have evolved ways of retaining accurate information. Given this, human initiative and experimentation may help account for the faster growth of complexity.

Notably, a number of successful businesses insist that their new plants or franchises should 'copy exactly' established procedures and routines. Given the importance of the faithful replication of information in evolving systems, this line of argument suggests that practitioners should be cautious about radical change in business organisations (Hodgson 2011). Experimentation should be cautious and not disregard acquired knowledge.

9 Evolutionary Understandings of Human Agency

Emphatically, the application of generalized Darwinian principles outlined in the preceding section does not rely on any conflation of social and biological phenomena. Instead, the argument is that some core, abstract, overarching principles apply to populations of *both* social and biological entities, despite the important differences between the nature of those entities and the big differences in the detailed mechanisms involved.

Generalized Darwinism does not entail biological reductionism, where social phenomena are explained wholly in terms of biology. The applicability of generalized Darwinian principles in this manner is entirely independent of the assumed influence of human biology on society, or on the degree of interaction between our biological and social natures.

But it would be rash to assume that human biology has no influence whatsoever on the nature of human society, or on human capacities or motivations. Once we accept the possibility of interaction between (or 'co-evolution' of) our social and biological natures, we open up a further line of enquiry that is logically independent of generalized Darwinism but also learns from Darwinian principles.

The bibliometric analysis of Hodgson and Lamberg (2018) shows that this line of enquiry has been largely avoided by evolutionary economists, with rare notable exceptions such as Witt (1992, 2003) and Bowles and Gintis (2011). But as J. W. Stoelhorst (2014) argued lucidly, modern developments in evolutionary anthropology, evolutionary psychology, and elsewhere are of major significance for the understanding of human capacities and behaviour (Boyd and Richerson 1985, Cosmides and Tooby 1994a, 1994b, Sober and Wilson 1998, Buss 1999, Hammerstein 2003, Richerson and Boyd 2004, De Waal 2006, Joyce 2006, Bowles and Gintis 2011, Haidt 2012).

From the nineteenth century and until recently, economics was dominated by the assumption of the self-interested, utility-maximizing individual. In the same crucial year, William Stanley Jevons (1871) and Carl Menger (1871), placed individual self-interest at the foundation of economics. Three years later, Léon Walras (1874) built neoclassical general equilibrium analysis upon a similar assumption of self-interest. But in the same year as the works by Jevons and Menger, Darwin (1871) published a contrasting and evolutionary explanation of cooperative solidarity and morality, which took over one hundred years to be confirmed broadly by theoretical and empirical research.

The modern versions of these Darwinian arguments offer a major challenge to some core assumptions in mainstream economics. Both pure self-interest and utility maximisation are questioned. It is remarkable that these arguments have so far been little used by evolutionary economists.

Let us first consider the substantial evidence against pure self-interest, with 'self-regarding preferences' when agents are interested in their own gain only. Numerous experiments with the Prisoner's Dilemma game have shown that many people do not defect, even when players are anonymous and the game is played once. In an analysis of thirty-seven different studies involving 130 experiments from 1958 to 1992, David Sally (1995) found an overall rate of cooperation of 47.4 per cent of the entire pooled sample.

It is important to distinguish between Prisoner's Dilemma experiments with a finite and an indefinite number of repeated plays. Using indefinite repeated plays of the Prisoner's Dilemma, Robert Axelrod (1984) famously demonstrated the strength of a 'tit-for-tat' strategy, where cooperation is met by a subsequent cooperation and defection punished by a subsequent defection. 'Tit-for-tat' won in a tournament with leading game theorists and mathematicians as players.

In a Public Goods game, individuals in a group (of say ten) are each given (say) $10 and offered the choice of keeping the money for themselves or investing it for the public good. All the money invested is multiplied by (say) two and distributed equally to all the members of the group, whether they contributed or not. If everyone contributes then each person will receive $20. If only one contributes, then she will receive $2. If no one contributes, each member gets $10. A payoff maximizer will invest nothing because of the risk that less than five people will contribute. In the Nash equilibrium, there is no investor, and everyone takes $10. By contrast, Robyn Dawes and Richard

Thaler (1988, p. 189) noted that in a series of experiments about half the participants contributed. No subsequent experimental study confirms the Nash prediction of an overall zero contribution.

There is an enormous amount of experimental evidence to undermine the idea that individuals are generally self-interested, payoff maximizers (e.g., Bowles and Gintis 2005, 2011, Camerer 2003, Camerer and Fehr 2006, Gintis *et al.* 2005, Gowdy 2004, Henrich *et al.* 2001, 2004). This evidence is so overwhelming that many economists have abandoned self-interested 'economic man' and joined in the quest for an enriched conception of human motivation. Much of this work uses evolutionary theory and insights from the analysis of gene-culture co-evolution.

One of the key building blocks in this literature is the idea of group selection (Sober and Wilson 1998, Bergstrom 2002, Wilson 2002, Henrich 2004, Hodgson and Knudsen 2010, Bowles and Gintis 2011). Again a coherent account of this idea relies on something like the distinction between replicators and interactors. Then, in turn, the distinction between two types of replicator is vital to understand the difference between 'genetic group selection' and 'cultural group selection' (Henrich 2004). In both cases, both groups and individuals are interactors, and both are potential objects of selection. Group selection results from competition between groups, and some groups have a greater capacity to survive and replicate than others. Genetic group selection focuses on the process by which group selection leads to changes in the gene pool of the entire population. Cultural group selection focuses on the process by which group selection leads to changes in the pool of habits, customs, or routines in the entire population.

The existence and extent of any kind of group selection is an empirical matter. Genetic group selection is undermined when individual migration between groups and other processes diminish the variation between groups. If inter-group migration were unbounded and extensive, then the mixed-up outcome would be much less variation of individual characteristics between groups than within groups themselves, and the variation within groups would approach the variation in the population as a whole. In these circumstances the groups would have few differentiating features, and genetic group selection would be undermined. By contrast, if migration is constrained, then genetic differences between groups can be maintained. This is a necessary but not sufficient condition for genetic group selection to occur.

The power of genetic group selection as a force depends on the genetic variation between groups being greater than the genetic variation within groups. If the difference is equalized through inter-group migration and mixing, then genetic group selection is eliminated.

The mechanisms of genetic transmission are quite different from those concerning cultural transmission. A key difference is that many of us have strong dispositions to conform to others. In this way, culture spreads through a group and helps lay down habits and customs of conformity, solidarity, and obedience. Individuals can change their cultural propensities as they adapt to a culture, but their genes remain mostly fixed. Consequently, culture can sometimes overcome the effects of migration, mixing, and diminished variation between groups.

The power of cultural group selection as a force depends on the cultural variation between groups being greater than the culture variation within groups. Because of powerful forces of conformity within groups and enduring variation between groups, cultural group selection is thought to be potentially more powerful than genetic group selection (Boyd and Richerson 1985, Henrich 2004, Hodgson and Knudsen 2010).

As Darwin (1871) himself argued, group selection leads to the development of individual habits and cultural traits that enhance the chances of survival of the group. Among these are dispositions that help members of the group to cooperate and work together. Accordingly, moral bonds and norms of sharing and cooperation develop as a result of cultural group selection (Sober and Wilson 1998, Wilson 2002, Boehm 2012). The logic of cultural group selection leads to varied individuals that have mixtures of moral, cooperative, and selfish motivations.

But as well as challenging the idea of self-interested 'economic man', evolutionary theory and experimental evidence also question the idea that the utility-maximizing model should be retained, even with preferences that are 'other-regarding' in that they take into account the perceived satisfaction of others as well. Such models with 'other-regarding' preferences have been used to model versions of altruism and cooperative behaviour (Bowles and Gintis 2011). But utility maximisation and preference functions are still assumed.

The assumption of utility maximisation (in any form) has long been criticised by Amartya Sen (1977, 1987) and others on the grounds that individual motivation is modular and more complex. Even if we can fit behaviour into an 'other-regarding' preference function, this does not mean that it is adequately explained by the maximisation of a single variable called utility. Darwinian evolutionary thinking adds more force to this argument.

Morality, as understood by leading moral philosophers, cannot be incorporated into models based on individual utility maximization, even with 'social' or 'other-regarding' preferences (Hare 1952, Mackie 1977, Joyce 2006). This is because morality is about 'doing the right thing', even if it would otherwise not be the preferred option. Moral judgments are inescapable and cannot be reduced to mere preferences. Digging deeper into the evolutionary and cultural origins of our motives leads us to the issue of morality. Moral motives have evolutionary origins and are sustained through interaction with others: morality is a social as well as an individual phenomenon.

Humans have moral capacities, but we are also self-interested. Evolution has provided us with instincts that trigger our moral development in suitable sociocultural settings. By contrast, basic instincts such as hunger and lust can be spurs to egoism. Through our socialization we typically develop into complex personalities in which biologically inherited impulses are extended or constrained to different degrees and in different ways.

The diverse inner impulses that we bring into the world may come into conflict as our personality develops in the institutional settings of parental care, peer group interaction, and organized education. These settings have major effects on how the moral and self-interested aspects of our personalities develop. Given our declining potential for adaptation as we get older, the earliest years are the most formative.

While accepting that individuals have multifaceted personalities, the mistake of influential neoclassical economists was to assume that in the economic sphere self-interest was overwhelming, and our altruistic and moral tendencies could be ignored as we entered the world of contract and business (Jevons 1871, Edgeworth 1881, Wicksteed 1910). Going a step further, writers such as Gary Becker (1976) claimed that utility maximization, developed in the neoclassical analysis of business life, applies generally to all social interactions.

But even firms and markets are unavoidably infused with moral considerations (Hobson 1929, McCloskey 2006, Zak 2008). These may be countered or developed by example or circumstance. If policymakers ignore our moral dispositions and concentrate on self-interest alone, then they could threaten the very fabric of a modern market economy (Schumpeter 1942).

The acknowledgement of moral motivation opens a large agenda for economists. It is highly relevant for the theory of the firm (Minkler 2008, Lopes *et al.* 2009, Hodgson 2013). It has been argued above that morality cannot be reduced to individual preferences or altruism. Consequently, economic policy is not just about maximizing satisfaction while ensuring that no one's utility is decreased; it should be about guiding and enhancing our moral dispositions. Especially from an evolutionary perspective, and even in the competitive world of modern business, there is no excuse for ignoring the evolution of moral systems and the moral motivations of economic agents.

This opens up a large but hitherto neglected area for evolutionary economists. Part of their challenge to mainstream economics would be to focus on its highly limited depiction of human motivation, centred on utility maximization. The kind of evolutionary thinking outlined in this section would be vital to help fill this gap.

10 Conclusion: Prospects for Evolutionary Economics

It has been established that modern evolutionary economics consists of a number of diverse approaches that nevertheless share some dispositions, concerns, and basic principles. The modern wave of evolutionary economics started in the 1980s, and in thirty years it has established a wide influence in both theoretical and policy areas. It is appropriate at this point to raise questions about the future of this school of thought.

This Element has emphasised the achievements of evolutionary economics while pointing to a few shared basic assumptions alongside a lack of theoretical consensus in other respects. Evolutionary economists assume a changing complex world that generates novelty. Agents therein have limited memories and cognitive capacities and assume that the rationality of others is similarly bounded (Hodgson 2007c). More recent work on generalized Darwinian principles points to different mechanisms of information retention and transmission between institutions, and the conditions of informational replication that have the potential to generate greater complexity (Hodgson and Knudsen 2010). Witt (2008) and other authors enhance this theoretical agenda of information transmission and complexity generation by pointing to the sources of novelty and examining the extent to which biological factors frame economic evolution. The overall promise here is for an economics that transcends static theory and accommodates a richer picture of the complexities and specificities of economic change. Is it possible that evolutionary economics will generate a theoretical paradigm to rival mainstream theory?

In response we must first note the point raised above concerning the contrast in style as well as content between much of evolutionary economics and mainstream economics (including game theory) as practiced in leading university departments of economics. As Witt (2008) and others have pointed out, there is little conversation and exchange of ideas between evolutionary and mainstream economics. This gap makes it difficult for evolutionary economics to influence economics as a whole. So far, it has had relatively little impact on university departments of economics. Instead, the influence of evolutionary economics has been more on research in business schools, on science and technology policy, and elsewhere. It is an open question whether evolutionary economics can continue to prosper as long as it remains largely separated from departments of economics in leading universities. Given that this separation is going to be very difficult to reverse, some thought should be given to alternative strategies for providing evolutionary economics with an institutional home within academia.

A second issue, also addressed above, is whether the lack of an explicit and openly shared set of core theoretical principles is an impediment to the future development of evolutionary economics. Although there are anthologies of essays and at least one journal devoted to evolutionary economics, there is no textbook. Such a textbook is unlikely to get off the ground unless there is a shared set of core theoretical ideas and not merely a shared set of modelling approaches and techniques. Neoclassical economics did not become established until Alfred Marshall (1890) synthesised the approach in his definitive *Principles of Economics.* The synthesis was not about modelling techniques: it was a comprehensive theoretical approach to the analysis of economic phenomena, organized and driven by core theoretical principles. One suggestion is that the principles of generalized Darwinism can fill the void. But the research programme involved in their elucidation is only in its infancy, and it is not yet clear how middle-range theory can be linked with this approach. Generalized Darwinism would require numerous empirical applications before it became a convincing framework for applied as well as theoretical work.

The spectre of Darwin raises a third (but strictly logically separate) issue: the extent to which evolutionary economics should take account of burgeoning research into the biological foundations of human behaviour. On this issue there is a division within evolutionary economics itself. While some leading evolutionary economists see biologically acquired dispositions as largely irrelevant to their work because culture is seen as sufficient to explain human attributes, others have indicated possible links and communalities (Veblen 1899, Witt 2003, Hodgson 2004a, Bowles and Gintis 2011). While evolutionary psychology has made prominent claims concerning the evolutionary origins of human attributes (Cosmides and Tooby 1994a, 1994b, Buss 1999), most evolutionary economists have made little use of this material. There is also a large and rapidly growing literature on the biological foundations of altruism and morality (Sober and Wilson 1998, Hammerstein 2003, De Waal 2006, Joyce 2006, Bowles and Gintis 2011, Hodgson 2013b) to which evolutionary economists have paid only limited attention. One wonders – particularly with the word 'evolutionary' in its chosen description – how long some leading evolutionary economists can continue to overlook these impressive advances in our understanding of the interactions between biological and cultural phenomena.

In sum, it is difficult to establish a clear prognosis for evolutionary economics in the coming decades. What is clear, however, is that evolutionary economics is one of the most well-established and successful rivals to mainstream economics. And it still has enormous potential for further development.

References

Alchian, Armen A. (1950) 'Uncertainty, Evolution, and Economic Theory', *Journal of Political Economy*, **58**(2), June, pp. 211–22.

Aldrich, Howard E. (1999) *Organizations Evolving* (London: Sage).

Aldrich, Howard E., Geoffrey M. Hodgson, David L. Hull, Thorbjørn Knudsen, Joel Mokyr and Viktor J. Vanberg (2008) 'In Defence of Generalized Darwinism', *Journal of Evolutionary Economics*, **18**(5), October, pp. 577–96.

Aldrich, Howard E. and Ruef, Martin (2006) *Organizations Evolving*, second edition. (London: Sage).

Alexander, J. McKenzie (2007) *The Structural Evolution of Morality* (Cambridge: Cambridge University Press).

Arrow, Kenneth J. (1995) 'Viewpoint: the Future', *Science*, **267**, 17 March, p. 1617.

Axelrod, Robert M. (1984) *The Evolution of Cooperation* (New York: Basic Books).

Axelrod, Robert M. (1986) 'An Evolutionary Approach to Norms', *American Political Science Review*, 80(4), December, pp. 1095–111.

Ayres, Clarence E. (1932) *Huxley* (New York: Norton).

Becker, Gary S. (1976) *The Economic Approach to Human Behavior* (Chicago: University of Chicago Press).

Bergstrom, Theodore C. (2002) 'Evolution of Social Behavior: Individual and Group Selection', *Journal of Economic Perspectives*, **16**(2), Spring, pp. 67–88.

Bicchieri, Cristina (2006) *The Grammar of Society* (Cambridge and New York: Cambridge University Press).

Binmore, Kenneth and Samuelson, Larry (1994) 'An Economist's Perspective on the Evolution of Norms', *Journal of Institutional and Theoretical Economics*, **150**(1), March, pp. 45–63.

Blau, Peter J. (1994) *The Organization of Academic Work* (New Brunswick, NJ: Transaction).

Blaug, Mark (1997) 'Ugly Currents in Modern Economics', *Options Politiques*, **18**(17), September, pp. 3–8. Reprinted in Mäki, Uskali (ed.) (2002) *Fact and Fiction in Economics: Models, Realism and Social Construction* (Cambridge and New York: Cambridge University Press).

Blaug, Mark (1999) 'The Formalist Revolution or What Happened to Orthodox Economics After World War II?', in Backhouse, Roger E. and Creedy, John (eds.) (1999) *From Classical Economics to the Theory of the Firm: Essays in Honour of D. P. O'Brien* (Cheltenham: Edward Elgar), pp. 257–80.

Boehm, Christopher (2012) *Moral Origins: the Evolution of Virtue, Altruism and Shame* (New York: Basic Books).

Boulding, Kenneth E. (1981) *Evolutionary Economics* (Beverly Hills, CA: Sage Publications).

Bowles, Samuel and Gintis, Herbert (eds.) (2005) *Moral Sentiments and Material Interests: the Foundations of Cooperation in Economic Life* (Cambridge: Massachusetts Institute of Technology Press).

Bowles, Samuel and Gintis, Herbert (2011) *A Cooperative Species: Human Reciprocity and Its Evolution* (Princeton, NJ: Princeton University Press).

Boyd, Robert and Richerson, Peter J. (1985) *Culture and the Evolutionary Process* (Chicago: University of Chicago Press).

Breslin, Dermot (2011) 'Reviewing a Generalized Darwinist Approach to Studying Socio-Economic Change', *International Journal of Management Reviews*, 13(2), pp. 218–35.

Bunge, Mario A. (1959) *Causality: the Place of the Causal Principle in Modern Science* (Cambridge, MA: Harvard University Press).

Buss, David M. (1999) *Evolutionary Psychology: the New Science of the Mind* (Needham Heights, MA: Allyn and Bacon).

Camic, Charles and Hodgson, Geoffrey M. (eds.) (2011) *Essential Writings of Thorstein Veblen* (London and New York: Routledge).

Camerer, Colin (2003) *Behavioral Game Theory: Experiments in Strategic Interaction* (Princeton, NJ: Princeton University Press).

Camerer, Colin F. and Fehr, Ernst (2006) 'When Does "Economic Man" Dominate Social Behavior?' *Science*, **311**, 6 January, pp. 47–52.

Campbell, Donald T. (1965) 'Variation, Selection and Retention in Sociocultural Evolution', in Barringer, H. R., Blanksten, G. I. and Mack, R. W. (eds.), *Social Change in Developing Areas: a Reinterpretation of Evolutionary Theory* (Cambridge, MA: Schenkman), pp. 19–49.

Case, Donald O. and Higgins, Georgeann M. (2000) 'How Can We Investigate Citation Behavior? A Study of Reasons for Citing Literature in Communication', *Journal of the American Society for Information Science and Technology*, 51(7), pp. 635–45.

Coase, Ronald H. (1937) 'The Nature of the Firm', *Economica*, 4, New Series, November, pp. 386–405.

Cohen, Wesley M. and Levinthal, Daniel A. (1990) 'Absorptive Capacity: a New Perspective on Learning and Innovation', *Administrative Science Quarterly*, 35(1), pp. 128–52.

Cordes, Christian (2006) 'Darwinism in Economics: from Analogy to Continuity', *Journal of Evolutionary Economics*, **16**(5), December, pp. 529–41.

Cosmides, Leda and Tooby, John (1994a) 'Beyond Intuition and Instinct Blindness: towards an Evolutionary Rigorous Cognitive Science', *Cognition*, **50**(1–3), April–June, pp. 41–77.

Cosmides, Leda and Tooby, John (1994b) 'Better than Rational: Evolutionary Psychology and the Invisible Hand', *American Economic Review (Papers and Proceedings)*, **84**(2), May, pp. 327–32.

Crane, Diana (1972) *Invisible Colleges. Diffusion of Knowledge in Scientific Communities* (Chicago: University of Chicago Press).

Cyert, Richard M. and March, James G. (1963) *A Behavioral Theory of the Firm* (Englewood Cliffs, NJ: Prentice-Hall).

Cziko, Gary (1995) *Without Miracles: Universal Selection Theory and the Second Darwinian Revolution* (Cambridge: Massachusetts Institute of Technology Press).

Darwin, Charles R. (1859) *On the Origin of Species by Means of Natural Selection, or the Preservation of Favoured Races in the Struggle for Life* (London: Murray).

Darwin, Charles R. (1871) *The Descent of Man, and Selection in Relation to Sex*, 2 vols. (London: Murray and New York: Hill).

Dawes, Robyn M. and Thaler, Richard H. (1988) 'Anomalies: Cooperation', *Journal of Economic Perspectives*, **2**(3), Summer, pp. 187–97.

Dawkins, Richard (1986) *The Blind Watchmaker*. Harlow: Longman.

De Waal, Frans B. M. (2006) *Primates and Philosophers: How Morality Evolved* (Princeton, NJ: Princeton University Press).

Degler, Carl N. (1991) *In Search of Human Nature: the Decline and Revival of Darwinism in American Social Thought* (Oxford and New York: Oxford University Press).

Dennett, Daniel C. (1995) *Darwin's Dangerous Idea: Evolution and the Meanings of Life* (London and New York: Allen Lane, and Simon and Schuster).

Dollimore, Denise E. and Hodgson, Geoffrey M. (2014) 'Four Essays on Economic Evolution: an Introduction', *Journal of Evolutionary Economics*, 24(1), January, pp. 1–10.

Dopfer, Kurt, Foster, John and Potts, Jason (2004) 'Micro-Meso-Macro', *Journal of Evolutionary Economics*, 14(3), pp. 263–79.

Dosi, Giovanni (1982) 'Technological Paradigms and Technological Trajectories: a Suggested Interpretation of the Determinants and Directions of Technical Change', *Research Policy*, 11(3), pp. 147–62.

Dosi, Giovanni, Freeman, Christopher, Nelson, Richard, Silverberg, Gerald and Soete, Luc L. G. (eds.) (1988) *Technical Change and Economic Theory* (London: Pinter).

Dosi, Giovanni, Levinthal, Daniel A. and Marengo, Luigi (2003) 'Bridging Contested Terrain: Linking Incentive-Based and Learning Perspectives on Organizational Evolution', *Industrial and Corporate Change*, **12**(2), pp. 413–36.

Dosi, Giovanni, Marsili Orietta, Orsenigo, Luigi and Salvatore, Roberta (1995) 'Technological Regimes, Selection and Market Structures', *Small Business Economics*, **7**, pp. 411–36

Dosi, Giovanni and Metcalfe, J. Stanley (1991) 'On Some Notions of Irreversibility in Economics', in Saviotti, Pier Paolo and Metcalfe, J. Stanley (eds.) (1991) *Evolutionary Theories of Economic and Technological Change: Present Status and Future Prospects* (Reading: Harwood), pp. 133–59.

Dunning, John H. (1989) 'The Study of International Business: a Plea for a More Interdisciplinary Approach', *Journal of International Business Studies*, 20(3), Fall, pp. 411–36.

Economist (1996) 'Dons and Dollars', *The Economist*, July 20, pp. 53–4.

Edgeworth, Francis Y. (1881) *Mathematical Psychics: an Essay on the Application of Mathematics to the Moral Sciences* (London: Kegan Paul).

Fletcher, Jeffrey A. and Zwick, Martin (2007). "The Evolution of Altruism: Game Theory in Multilevel Selection and Inclusive Fitness," *Journal of Theoretical Biology*, 245(1), pp. 26–36.

Foss, Nicolai Juul (1994), 'Realism and Evolutionary Economics', *Journal of Social and Evolutionary Systems*, **17**(1), 21–40.

Foster, John (1997) 'The Analytical Foundations of Evolutionary Economics: from Biological Analogy to Economic Self-Organisation', *Structural Change and Economic Dynamics*, **8**(4), October, pp. 427–51.

Friedman, Milton (1953) 'The Methodology of Positive Economics', in M. Friedman, *Essays in Positive Economics* (Chicago: University of Chicago Press), pp. 3–43.

Geisendorf, Sylvie (2009) 'The Economic Concept of Evolution – Self-Organization or Universal Darwinism?' *Journal of Economic Methodology*, **16**(4), December, pp. 359–73.

Georgescu-Roegen, Nicholas (1971) *The Entropy Law and the Economic Process* (Cambridge, MA: Harvard University Press).

Gintis, Herbert (2003) 'The Hitchhiker's Guide to Altruism: Genes, Culture, and the Internalization of Norms', *Journal of Theoretical Biology*, 220(4), pp. 407–18.

Gintis, Herbert, Bowles, Samuel, Boyd, Robert and Fehr, Ernst (eds.) (2003) 'Explaining Altruistic Behavior in Humans', *Evolution and Human Behavior*, 24(2), pp. 153–72.

Gintis, Herbert, Bowles, Samuel, Boyd, Robert and Fehr, Ernst (eds.) (2005) *Moral Sentiments and Material Interests: the Foundations of Cooperation in Economic Life* (Cambridge: Massachusetts Institute of Technology Press).

Godfrey-Smith, Peter (2009) *Darwinian Populations and Natural Selection* (Oxford: Oxford University Press).

Gowdy, John M. (2004) 'Altruism, Evolution, and Welfare Economics', *Journal of Economic Behavior and Organization*, **53**(1), February, pp. 69–73.

Hahn, Frank H. (1991) 'The Next Hundred Years', *Economic Journal*, **101**(1), January, pp. 47–50.

Haidt, Jonathan (2012) *The Righteous Mind: Why Good People are Divided by Politics and Religion* (London: Penguin).

Haltiwanger, John and Waldman, Michael (1985) 'Rational Expectations and the Limits of Rationality: an Analysis of Heterogeneity', *American Economic Review* 75.3: 159–73.

Hammerstein, Peter (ed.) (2003) *Genetic and Cultural Evolution of Cooperation* (Cambridge: Massachusetts Institute of Technology Press).

Hannan, Michael T. and Freeman, John (1989) *Organizational Ecology* (Cambridge, MA: Harvard University Press).

Hare, Richard M. (1952) *The Language of Morals* (Oxford: Oxford University Press).

Hargreaves Heap, Shaun P. and Varoufakis, Yanis (1995) *Game Theory: a Critical Introduction*, Routledge, London and New York.

Hayek, Friedrich A. (1967) 'Notes on the Evolution of Systems of Rules of Conduct', from Hayek, Friedrich A. (1967) *Studies in Philosophy, Politics and Economics* (London: Routledge and Kegan Paul), pp. 66–81.

Hayek, Friedrich A. (1948) *Individualism and Economic Order* (London and Chicago: George Routledge and University of Chicago Press).

Hayek, Friedrich A. (1973) *Law, Legislation and Liberty; Volume 1: Rules and Order* (London: Routledge and Kegan Paul).

Hayek, Friedrich A. (1979) *Law, Legislation and Liberty; Volume 3: The Political Order of a Free People* (London: Routledge and Kegan Paul).

Hayek, Friedrich A. (1988) *The Fatal Conceit: the Errors of Socialism. The Collected Works of Friedrich August Hayek, Vol. I*, ed. William W. Bartley III (London: Routledge).

Henrich, Joseph (2004) 'Cultural Group Selection, Coevolutionary Processes and Large-Scale Cooperation', *Journal of Economic Behavior and Organization*, **53**(1), February, pp. 3–35.

Henrich, Joseph, Boyd, Robert, Bowles, Samuel, Camerer, Colin, Fehr, Ernst, Gintis, Herbert and McElreath, Richard (2001) 'In Search of Homo Economicus: Behavioral Experiments in 15 Small-Scale Societies', *American Economic Review (Papers and Proceedings)*, **91**(2), May, pp. 73–84.

Henrich, Joseph, Boyd, Robert, Bowles, Samuel, Camerer, Colin, Fehr, Ernst, and Gintis, Herbert (2004) *Foundations of Human Sociality: Economic*

Experiments and Ethnographic Evidence from Fifteen Small-Scale Societies (Oxford and New York: Oxford University Press).

Higher Education Student Statistics UK (2018) *HESA*, 'Higher Education Student Statistics: UK, 2016/17 – Qualifications Achieved'. www .hesa.ac.uk/news/11–01-2018/sfr247-higher-education-student-statistics /qualifications. (Retrieved 14 July 2018.)

Hobson, John A. (1929) *Wealth and Life: a Study in Values* (London: Macmillan).

Hodgson, Geoffrey M. (1993) *Economics and Evolution: Bringing Life Back Into Economics* (Cambridge, UK and Ann Arbor, MI: Polity Press and University of Michigan Press).

Hodgson, Geoffrey M. (1997) 'The Ubiquity of Habits and Rules', *Cambridge Journal of Economics*, **21**(6), November, pp. 663–84.

Hodgson, Geoffrey M. (2004a) *The Evolution of Institutional Economics: Agency, Structure and Darwinism in American Institutionalism* (London and New York: Routledge).

Hodgson, Geoffrey M. (2004b) 'Darwinism, Causality and the Social Sciences', *Journal of Economic Methodology*, **11**(2), June, pp. 175–94.

Hodgson, Geoffrey M. (2007a) 'The Revival of Veblenian Institutional Economics', *Journal of Economic Issues*, **41**(2), June, pp. 325–40.

Hodgson, Geoffrey M. (2007b) 'Taxonomizing the Relationship between Biology and Economics: a Very Long Engagement', *Journal of Bioeconomics*, **9**(2), August, pp. 169–85.

Hodgson, Geoffrey M. (2007c) 'Evolutionary and Institutional Economics as the New Mainstream?', *Evolutionary and Institutional Economics Review*, **4**(1), September 2007, pp. 7–25.

Hodgson, Geoffrey M. (2009) 'On the Institutional Foundations of Law: the Insufficiency of Custom and Private Ordering', *Journal of Economic Issues*, **43**(1), March, pp. 143–66.

Hodgson, Geoffrey M. (2011) 'Organizational Evolution versus the Cult of Change', *Corporate Finance Review*, January–February, 16(1), pp. 5–10.

Hodgson, Geoffrey M. (2013a) 'Understanding Organizational Evolution: toward a Research Agenda using Generalized Darwinism', *Organization Studies*, 34(7), July 2013, pp. 973–92.

Hodgson, Geoffrey M. (2013b) *From Pleasure Machines to Moral Communities: an Evolutionary Economics without Homo Economicus* (Chicago: University of Chicago Press).

Hodgson, Geoffrey M. (2014) 'The Evolution of Morality and the End of Economic Man', *Journal of Evolutionary Economics*, 24(1), January, pp. 83–106.

Hodgson, Geoffrey M. (2015) *Conceptualizing Capitalism: Institutions, Evolution, Future* (Chicago: University of Chicago Press).

Hodgson, Geoffrey M. (2019) *Is There a Future for Heterodox Economics? Institutions, Ideology and a Scientific Community* (Cheltenham, UK and Northampton, MA: Edward Elgar).

Hodgson, Geoffrey M., Herman, Stephen and Dollimore, Denise E. (2017) 'Adaptability and Survival in Small- and Medium-Sized Firms', *Industrial and Corporate Change*, published online.

Hodgson, Geoffrey M. and Huang, Kainan (2012) 'Evolutionary Game Theory and Evolutionary Economics: Are They Different Species?' *Journal of Evolutionary Economics*, 22, pp. 345–66.

Hodgson, Geoffrey M. and Knudsen, Thorbjørn (2006) 'Why We Need a Generalized Darwinism: and Why a Generalized Darwinism Is Not Enough', *Journal of Economic Behavior and Organization*, **61**(1), September, pp. 1–19.

Hodgson, Geoffrey M. and Knudsen, Thorbjørn (2010) *Darwin's Conjecture: the Search for General Principles of Social and Economic Evolution* (Chicago: University of Chicago Press).

Hodgson, Geoffrey M. and Lamberg, Juha-Antti (2018) 'The Past and Future of Evolutionary Economics: Some Reflections Based on New Bibliometric Evidence', *Evolutionary and Institutional Economics Review*, 15(1), pp. 167–87.

Hodgson, Geoffrey M. and Stoelhorst, J. W. (2014) 'Introduction to the Special Issue on the Future of Institutional and Evolutionary Economics', *Journal of Institutional Economics*, 10(4), December, pp. 513–40.

Hull, David L. (1988) *Science as a Process: an Evolutionary Account of the Social and Conceptual Development of Science* (Chicago: University of Chicago Press).

Hurd, Peter L. (1995) 'Communication in Discrete Action-Response Games', *Journal of Theoretical Biology*, 174(2), pp. 217–22.

Jäger, Gerhard (2008) 'Evolutionary Stability Conditions for Signalling Games with Costly Signals', *Journal of Theoretical Biology*, 253(2), pp. 131–41.

Jevons, William Stanley (1871) *The Theory of Political Economy* (London: Macmillan).

Jones, Lamar B. (1995) 'C. E. Ayres's Reliance on T. H. Huxley: Did Darwin's Bulldog Bite?' *American Journal of Economics and Sociology*, 54(4), October, pp. 413–20.

Joyce, Richard (2006) *The Evolution of Morality* (Cambridge: Massachusetts Institute of Technology Press).

Kameda, Tatsuya and Nakanishi, Daisuke (2003) 'Does Social/Cultural Learning Increase Human Adaptability? Rogers's Question Revisited', *Evolution and Human Behavior*, **24**(4), pp. 242–60.

Kauffman, Stuart A. (1993) *The Origins of Order: Self-Organization and Selection in Evolution* (Oxford and New York: Oxford University Press).

Kauffman, Stuart A. (1995) *At Home in the Universe: the Search for Laws of Self-Organization and Complexity* (Oxford and New York: Oxford University Press).

Kitcher, Philip (1993) *The Advancement of Science: Science without Legend, Objectivity without Illusions* (Oxford and New York: Oxford University Press).

Klaes, Matthias (2004) 'Evolutionary Economics: in Defence of "Vagueness"', *Journal of Economic Methodology*, **11**(3), September, pp. 359–76.

Klamer, Arjo and Colander, David (1990) *The Making of an Economist* (Boulder: Westview Press).

Knorr-Cetina, Karin D. (1981) *The Manufacture of Knowledge: an Essay on the Constructivist and Contextual Nature of Science* (Oxford: Pergamon).

Koestler, Arthur (1964) *The Act of Creation* (London: Hutchinson).

Kornai, János (1971) *Anti-Equilibrium: on Economic Systems Theory and the Tasks of Research* (Amsterdam: North-Holland). Reprinted 1991 (New York: Augustus Kelley).

Krueger, Anne O. (1991) 'Report on the Commission on Graduate Education in Economics', *Journal of Economic Literature*, **29**(3), September, pp. 1035–53.

Kuhn, Thomas S. (1962) *The Structure of Scientific Revolutions* (Chicago: University of Chicago Press).

Lakatos, Imre (1970) 'Falsification and the Methodology of Scientific Research Programmes', in Lakatos, Imre and Musgrave, Alan (eds.) (1970) *Criticism and the Growth of Knowledge* (Cambridge: Cambridge University Press) pp. 91–195.

Lamarck, Jean Baptiste de (1963) *Zoological Philosophy: an Exposition with Regard to the Natural History of Animals*, translated from the 1st French edn. of 1809 (New York: Hafner).

Laudan, Larry (1977) *Progress and Its Problems: towards a Theory of Scientific Growth* (London: Routledge and Kegan Paul).

Levinthal, Daniel A. (1992) 'Surviving Schumpeterian Environments: an Evolutionary Perspective', *Industrial and Corporate Change*, 1, pp. 427–43.

Lewin, Arie Y. and Mitchell P. Koza (2001) 'Editorial', *Organization Studies*, 22(6), November, pp. v–xii.

Lewin, Arie Y. and Volberda, Henk W. (1999) 'Prolegomena on Coevolution: a Framework for Research on Strategy and New Organizational Forms', *Organization Science*, 10(5), September–October, pp. 519–34.

Lewontin, Richard C. (1961) 'Evolution and the Theory of Games', *Journal of Theoretical Biology*, 1, pp. 382–403.

Lopes, Helena, Ana C. Santos and Nuno Teles (2009) 'The Motives for Cooperation in Work Organisations', *Journal of Institutional Economics*, 5(3), December, pp. 259–88.

Lucio-Arias, Diana and Leydesdorff, Loet (2008) 'Main-Path Analysis and Path-Dependent Transitions in *HistCite*™-Based Historiograms', *Journal of the American Society for Information Science and Technology*, 59(12), pp. 1948–62.

Lundvall, Bengt-Åke (ed.) (1992) *National Systems of Innovation: towards a Theory of Innovation and Interactive Learning* (London: Pinter).

Mackie, John Leslie (1977) *Ethics: Inventing Right and Wrong* (Harmondsworth: Penguin).

Malerba, Franco, Nelson, Richard R., Orsenigo, Luigi and Winter, Sidney G. (1999) '"History Friendly" Models of Industry Evolution: the Computer Industry', *Industrial and Corporate Change*, 8(1), pp. 3–40.

Malerba, Franco and Orsenigo, Luigi (2002) 'Innovation and Market Structure in the Dynamics of the Pharmaceutical Industry and Biotechnology: towards a History-Friendly Model' *Industrial and Corporate Change*, 11(4), pp. 667–703.

March, James G. (1991). 'Exploration and Exploitation in Organizational Learning', *Organization Science*, 2(1), pp. 71–87.

March, James G. and Simon, Herbert A. (1958) *Organizations* (New York: Wiley).

Marshall, Alfred (1890) *Principles of Economics: An Introductory Volume* (London: Macmillan).

Marx, Karl (1976) *Capital*, vol. 1, translated by Ben Fowkes from the fourth German edition of 1890 (Harmondsworth: Pelican).

Maynard Smith, John (1972) 'Game Theory and the Evolution of Fighting', in Maynard Smith, John, *On Evolution* (Edinburgh: Edinburgh University Press) pp. 8–28.

Maynard Smith, John (1982) *Evolutionary Game Theory* (Cambridge: Cambridge University Press).

Maynard Smith, John and Price, George R. (1973) 'The Logic of Animal Conflict', *Nature*, 246, pp. 15–18.

Mayr, Ernst (1991) *One Long Argument: Charles Darwin and the Genesis of Modern Evolutionary Thought* (Cambridge, MA and London: Harvard University Press and Allen Lane).

McCloskey, Deirdre N. (2006) *The Bourgeois Virtues: Ethics for an Age of Commerce* (Chicago: Chicago University Press).

McKelvey, Maureen (1996) *Evolutionary Innovations: the Business of Biotechnology* (Oxford: Oxford University Press).

Menger, Carl (1871) *Grundsätze der Volkwirtschaftslehre*, 1st edn. (Tübingen: J. C. B. Mohr). Published in English in 1981 as *Principles of Economics* (New York: New York University Press).

Metcalfe, J. Stanley (1998) *Evolutionary Economics and Creative Destruction* (London and New York: Routledge).

Minkler, Lanse P. (2008) *Integrity and Agreement: Economics When Principles Also Matter* (Ann Arbor, MI: University of Michigan Press).

Murmann, Johann Peter (2003) *Knowledge and Competitive Advantage: the Coevolution of Firms, Technology and National Institutions* (Cambridge and New York: Cambridge University Press).

Murmann, Johann Peter, Aldrich, Howard E., Levinthal, Daniel and Winter, Sidney G. (2003) 'Evolutionary Thought in Management and Organization Theory at the Beginning of the New Millennium: a Symposium on the State of the Art and Opportunities for Future Research', *Journal of Management Inquiry*, **12**(1), March, pp. 22–40.

Nakahashi, Wataru (2007) 'The Evolution of Conformist Transmission in Social Learning when the Environment Changes Periodically', *Theoretical Population Biology*, 72(1), pp. 52–66.

National Centre for Education Statistics (2017) *Digest of Education Statistics*. https://nces.ed.gov/fastfacts/display.asp?id=37. (Retrieved 14 July 2018.)

Nelson, Richard R. (ed.) (1993) *National Innovation Systems: a Comparative Analysis* (Oxford: Oxford University Press).

Nelson, Richard R. (2008) 'Factors Affecting the Power of Technological Paradigms', *Industrial and Corporate Change*, 17(3), pp. 485–97.

Nelson, Richard R. and Winter, Sidney G. (1982) *An Evolutionary Theory of Economic Change* (Cambridge, MA: Harvard University Press).

Noam, Eli M. (1995) 'Electronics and the Dim Future of the University', *Science*, Vol. 270, October 13, pp. 247–9.

Nowak, Martin A., Joshua B. Plotkin and David C. Krakauer (1999) 'The Evolutionary Language Game', *Journal of Theoretical Biology*, 200(2), pp. 147–62.

Nowak, Martin A. and Sigmund, Karl (2005) 'Evolution of Indirect Reprocity', *Nature*, **437**, 27 October, pp. 1291–8.

Ostrom, Elinor (2000) 'Collective Action and the Evolution of Social Norms', *Journal of Economic Perspectives*, **14**(3), Summer, pp. 137–58.

Pawlowitsch, Christina (2007) 'Finite Populations Choose an Optimal Language', *Journal of Theoretical Biology*, 249(3), pp. 606–16.

Pawlowitsch, Christina (2008) 'Why Evolution Does Not Always Lead to an Optimal Signaling System', *Games and Economic Behavior*, 63(1), pp. 203–26.

Peirce, Charles Sanders (1958) *Selected Writings (Values in a Universe of Chance)*, edited with an introduction by Philip P. Wiener (New York: Doubleday).

Pessali, Huascar F. (2006) 'The Rhetoric of Oliver Williamson's Transaction Cost Economics', *Journal of Institutional Economics*, **2**(1), April, pp. 45–65.

Polanyi, Michael (1962) 'The Republic of Science: Its Political and Economic Theory', *Minerva*, 1, pp. 54–73.

Potts, Jason (2000) *The New Evolutionary Microeconomics: Complexity, Competence and Adaptive Behaviour* (Cheltenham: Edward Elgar).

Price, George R. (1970) 'Selection and Covariance', *Nature*, 227, pp. 520–1.

Price, George R. (1995) 'The Nature of Selection', *Journal of Theoretical Biology*, **175**, pp. 389–96.

Richards, Robert J. (1992) *The Meaning of Evolution: the Morphological Construction and Ideological Reconstruction of Darwin's Theory* (Chicago: University of Chicago Press).

Richerson, Peter J. and Boyd, Robert (2004) *Not by Genes Alone: How Culture Transformed Human Evolution* (Chicago: University of Chicago Press).

Richiardi, Matteo and Leombruni, Roberto (2005) 'Why Are Economists Sceptical about Agent-Based Simulations?' *Physica A*, 355(1), pp. 103–9.

Rizvi, S. Abu Turab (1994a) 'The Microfoundations Project in General Equilibrium Theory', *Cambridge Journal of Economics*, **18**(4), August, pp. 357–77.

Rizvi, S. Abu Turab (1994b) 'Game Theory to the Rescue?', *Contributions to Political Economy*, **13**, pp. 1–28.

Rutherford, Malcolm H. (2011) *The Institutionalist Movement in American Economics, 1918–1947: Science and Social Control* (Cambridge and New York: Cambridge University Press).

Sally, David (1995) 'Conversation and Cooperation in Social Dilemmas: a Meta-Analysis of Experiments from 1958–1992', *Rationality and Society*, **7**(1), pp. 58–92.

Sánchez, Angel and José A. Cuesta (2005) 'Altruism May Arise from Individual Selection', *Journal of Theoretical Biology*, 235(2), pp. 233–40.

Saviotti, Pier Paolo (1996) *Technological Evolution, Variety and the Economy* (Aldershot: Edward Elgar).

Schumpeter, Joseph A. (1934) *The Theory of Economic Development: An Inquiry into Profits, Capital, Credit, Interest, and the Business Cycle*, translated by Redvers Opie from the second German edition of 1926, first edition 1911 (Cambridge, MA: Harvard University Press).

Schumpeter, Joseph A. (1939) *Business Cycles: a Theoretical Statistical and Historical Analysis of the Capitalist Process*, 2 vols. (New York: McGraw-Hill).

Schumpeter, Joseph A. (1942) *Capitalism, Socialism and Democracy*, 1st edn. (London: George Allen and Unwin).

Sen, Amartya K. (1977) 'Rational Fools: a Critique of the Behavioral Foundations of Economic Theory', *Philosophy and Public Affairs*, **6**(4), pp. 317–44.

Sen, Amartya K. (1987) *On Ethics and Economics* (Oxford and New York: Basil Blackwell).

Silva, Sandra Tavares and Teixeira, Aurora A. C. (2009) 'On the Divergence of Evolutionary Research Paths in the Past 50 years: a Comprehensive Bibliometric Account', *Journal of Evolutionary Economics*, **19**(5), October, pp. 605–42.

Silverberg, Gerald, Dosi, Giovanni and Orsenigo, Luigi (1988) 'Innovation, Diversity and Diffusion: a Self-Organization Model', *Economic Journal*, 98(4), December, pp. 1032–54.

Simon, Herbert A. (1957) *Models of Man: Social and Rational. Mathematical Essays on Rational Human Behavior in a Social Setting* (New York: Wiley).

Skyrms, Brian (1996) *Evolution of the Social Contract* (Cambridge and New York: Cambridge University Press).

Skyrms, Brian (2004). *The Stag Hunt and the Evolution of Social Structure* (Cambridge and New York: Cambridge University Press).

Small, Henry (2004) 'On the Shoulders of Robert Merton: towards a Normative Theory of Citation', *Scientometrics*, 60(1), pp. 71–9.

Sober, Elliott and Wilson, David Sloan (1998) *Unto Others: the Evolution and Psychology of Unselfish Behavior* (Cambridge, MA: Harvard University Press).

Spencer, Herbert (1862) *First Principles* (London: Williams and Norgate).

Sperber, Dan (2000) 'An Objection to the Memetic Approach to Culture', in Aunger, Robert (ed.) (2000) *Darwinizing Culture: the Status of Memetics as a Science* (Oxford and New York: Oxford University Press), pp. 162–73.

Starkey, Ken and Madan, Paula (2001) 'Bridging the Relevance Gap: Aligning Stakeholders in the Future of Management Research', *British Journal of Management*, 12 (Supplement S1), December, pp. S3–S26.

Sterelny, Kim, Smith, Kelly C. and Dickison, Michael (1996) 'The Extended Replicator', *Biology and Philosophy*, **11**, pp. 377–403.

Stoelhorst, J. W. (2008) 'The Explanatory Logic and Ontological Commitments of Generalized Darwinism', *Journal of Economic Methodology*, **15**(4), December, pp. 343–63.

Stoelhorst, J. W. (2014) 'The Future of Evolutionary Economics Is in a Vision from the Past: a Comment on the Essays on Evolutionary Economics by Sidney Winter and Ulrich Witt', *Journal of Institutional Economics*, 10(4), December, pp. 665–82.

Sugden, Robert (1986) *The Economics of Rights, Co-operation and Welfare* (Oxford: Basil Blackwell).

Sugden, Robert (2000) 'Credible Worlds: the Status of Theoretical Models in Economics', *Journal of Economic Methodology*, **7**(1), March, pp. 1–31.

Usher, John M. and Evans, Martin G. (1996) 'Life and Death along Gasoline Alley: Darwinian and Lamarckian Processes in a Differentiating Population', *Academy of Management Journal*, **39**(5), October, pp. 1428–66.

Vanberg, Viktor J. (1986) 'Spontaneous Market Order and Social Rules: a Critique of F. A. Hayek's Theory of Cultural Evolution', *Economics and Philosophy*, 2(1), April, pp. 75–100.

Vanberg, Viktor J. (2004) 'The Rationality Postulate in Economics: Its Ambiguity, Its Deficiency and Its Evolutionary Alternative', *Journal of Economic Methodology* 11.1: 1–29.

Veblen, Thorstein B. (1898) 'Why Is Economics Not an Evolutionary Science?', *Quarterly Journal of Economics*, **12**(3), July, pp. 373–97. Reprinted in Camic and Hodgson (2011).

Veblen, Thorstein B. (1899) *The Theory of the Leisure Class: an Economic Study in the Evolution of Institutions* (New York: Macmillan).

Veblen, Thorstein B. (1906) 'The Socialist Economics of Karl Marx and His Followers I: the Theories of Karl Marx', *Quarterly Journal of Economics*, **20**(3), August, pp. 578–95. Reprinted in Camic and Hodgson (2011).

Veblen, Thorstein B. (1907) 'The Socialist Economics of Karl Marx and His Followers II: the Later Marxism', *Quarterly Journal of Economics*, **21**(1), February, pp. 299–322. Reprinted in Camic and Hodgson (2011).

Veblen, Thorstein B. (1919) *The Place of Science in Modern Civilisation and Other Essays* (New York: Huebsch).

Verspagen, Bart and Werker, Claudia (2003) 'The Invisible College of the Economics of Innovation and Technological Change', *Estudios de Economía Aplicada*, **21**(3), pp. 393–419.

Villena, Mauricio G. and Villena, Marcelo J. (2004) 'Evolutionary Game Theory and Thorstein Veblen's Evolutionary Economics: Is EGT Veblenian?', *Journal of Economic Issues*, **38**(3), September, pp. 585–610.

Wakano, Joe Yuichiro, Aoki, Kenichi and Feldman, Marcus W. (2004) 'Evolution of Social Learning: a Mathematical Analysis', *Theoretical Population Biology*, 66(3), pp. 249–58.

Wakano, Joe Yuichiro and Aoki, Kenichi (2006) 'A Mixed Strategy Model for the Emergence and Intensification of Social Learning in a Periodically Changing Natural Environment', *Theoretical Population Biology*, 70(4), pp. 486–97.

Walras, Léon (1874) *Éléments d'économie politique pure, ou théorie de la richesse sociale* (Lausanne: Rouge).

Weingart, Peter and Stehr, Nico (eds.) (2000) *Practicising Interdisciplinarity* (Toronto: University of Toronto Press).

Wenger, Etienne (1998) *Communities of Practice: Learning, Memory and Identity* (Cambridge: Cambridge University Press).

Wicksteed, Philip H. (1910) *The Commonsense of Political Economy, Including a Study of the Human Basis of Economic Law* (London: Macmillan).

Williamson, Oliver E. (1975) *Markets and Hierarchies: Analysis and Anti-Trust Implications: a Study in the Economics of Internal Organization* (New York: Free Press).

Williamson, Oliver E. (1985) *The Economic Institutions of Capitalism: Firms, Markets, Relational Contracting* (London and New York: Free Press and Macmillan).

Wilson, David Sloan (2002) *Darwin's Cathedral: Evolution, Religion, and the Nature of Society* (Chicago: University of Chicago Press).

Winter, Sidney G., Jr (1987) 'Natural Selection and Evolution', in Eatwell, John, Milgate, Murray and Newman, Peter (eds.) (1987) *The New Palgrave Dictionary of Economics* (London: Macmillan), vol. 3, pp. 614–17.

Witt, Ulrich (ed.) (1992) *Explaining Process and Change: Approaches to Evolutionary Economics*, Ann Arbor, MI: University of Michigan Press.

Witt, Ulrich (1997) 'Self-Organisation and Economics – What Is New?' *Structural Change and Economic Dynamics*, **8**, pp. 489–507.

Witt, Ulrich (2002) 'How Evolutionary Is Schumpeter's Theory of Economic Development?', *Industry and Innovation*, 9(1/2), pp. 7–22.

Witt, Ulrich (2003) *The Evolving Economy: Essays on the Evolutionary Approach to Economics* (Cheltenham, UK and Northampton, MA: Edward Elgar).

Witt, Ulrich (2008) 'What Is Specific about Evolutionary Economics?' *Journal of Evolutionary Economics*, **18**, pp. 547–75.

Zak, Paul J. (ed.) (2008) *Moral Markets: the Critical Role of Values in the Economy* (Princeton: Princeton University Press).

Zollman, Kevin J. S. (2005) 'Talking to Neighbors: the Evolution of Regional Meaning', *Philosophy of Science*, 72(1), pp. 69–85.

About the Author

Geoffrey M. Hodgson is a Professor in Management at Loughborough University London, UK. He is author of *Is There a Future for Heterodox Economics?* (2019), *Is Socialism Feasible?* (2019),*Wrong Turnings: How the Left Got Lost* (2018), *Conceptualizing Capitalism* (2015), *From Pleasure Machines to Moral Communities* (2013), *Darwin's Conjecture: The Search for General Principles of Social and Economic Evolution* (2010, with Thorbjørn Knudsen), *The Evolution of Institutional Economics* (2004), *How Economics Forgot History* (2001), several other books, and over 150 academic journal articles. He is Editor in Chief of the *Journal of Institutional Economics,* a Fellow of the Academy of Social Sciences, and a Fellow of the Royal Society of Arts. His website is www.geoffreymhodgson.uk.

Cambridge Elements ☰

Evolutionary Economics

John Foster
University of Queensland

John Foster is Emeritus Professor of Economics at the University of Queensland, Brisbane. He is Fellow of the Academy of Social Science in Australia; Life member of Clare Hall College, Cambridge; and Past President of the International J. A. Schumpeter Society. He is also Director of the Energy Economics and Management Group at UQ and Focal Leader for Renewable Energy at the Global Change Institute.

Jason Potts
RMIT University

Jason Potts is Professor of Economics at RMIT University, Melbourne. He is also an Adjunct Fellow at the Institute of Public Affairs. His research interests include technological change, economics of innovation, and economics of cities. He was the winner of the 2000 International Joseph A. Schumpeter Prize and has published over sixty articles and six books.

About the Series

The Cambridge Elements of Evolutionary Economics provides authoritative and up-to-date reviews of core topics and recent developments in the field. It includes state-of-the-art contributions on all areas in the field. The series is broadly concerned with questions of dynamics and change, with a particular focus on processes of entrepreneurship and innovation, industrial and institutional dynamics, and on patterns of economic growth and development.

Cambridge Elements ≡

Evolutionary Economics

Elements in the Series

CPSIA information can be obtained
at www.ICGtesting.com
Printed in the USA
LVHW081004211019
634838LV00013B/354/P